LIVING IN STYLE
NEW YORK

Edited by Vanessa Weiner von Bismarck
Texts by Jean Nayar

teNeues

Contents

Introduction

Vanessa Weiner von Bismarck

FEW CITIES ON earth are as diverse as this one, so it's hardly surprising that New York homes encompass an exceptional array of styles. The incredible mix of people from various countries who call this great city home means surprise is a constant ingredient. A magnet for creative, dynamic individuals in every sector, its streets and venues are charged with an eclectic energy. For everybody who lives here (whether a longtime resident or starry-eyed newcomer), New York offers the chance for people to create lives that are more vibrant and varied than just about anywhere else.

Just as it's hard to define a typical New Yorker, it's even harder to define a typical New York space—except that it'll probably be daring, original, and certainly not predictable. New Yorkers' love for culture and their passion for art can be equally well showcased in converted, industrial loft spaces, modernist penthouses, or traditional townhouses. Furthermore, the city itself is constantly in flux. Neighborhoods evolve and reconfigure themselves in a few short years. Since I've arrived in New York, for example, Chelsea has morphed from a sparsely populated art-focused outpost to one of the most desirable family neighborhoods by just adding a new school. Or take the Meatpacking District—once defined by butchers and delivery trucks—where today you can find the much talked about High Line and the wonderful bustle of the Chelsea Market. Or Brooklyn, which offers a seemingly endless array of new restaurants, cultural events, artists, and talented furniture makers.

Unlike many European cities I've lived in, New Yorkers give their design fantasies free reign. There's no conventional standard to adhere to or rules defining the way "it has to be." I find this freedom both refreshing and challenging. New Yorkers are unintimidated by color in their living spaces. They're also incredibly resourceful when it comes to architecture and finding ways to reinvent classic New York elements—such as turning a cast iron column into a stunning centerpiece for a bench. If that's not enough, they're unafraid to redefine the whole concept of an urban jungle by cultivating gardens up their interior and exterior walls.

Having lived here for fifteen years and now going through a major renovation myself, I'm learning firsthand that when it comes to interiors, the choices are truly endless, the talent plentiful. Whereas in many other places I had a design template to follow, here I'm on my own. It's exhilarating (and also a tiny bit terrifying) to be able to choose who you are, what your world should look like. Yet, isn't that willingness to create something extraordinary what New York is all about? You arrive here, you decide who you want to be, and then you go out and do your best to become that—just as many times and as frequently as you'd care to.

Einleitung
Vanessa Weiner von Bismarck

NUR WENIGE STÄDTE der Welt sind so vielfältig wie New York. So verwundert es kaum, dass auch die Häuser und Wohnungen ein außergewöhnliches Spektrum an Stilen aufweisen. Aufgrund der unglaublichen Mischung der aus vielen Ländern stammenden Menschen, die diese großartige Stadt ihr Zuhause nennen, ist die Überraschung ein fester Bestandteil von ihr. Da die Stadt kreative, dynamische Personen aus sämtlichen Bereichen magisch anzieht, sprühen die Straßen und Orte geradezu vor Energie. Für jeden, der hier wohnt (egal ob alteingesessen oder frisch hinzugezogen), bietet New York die Chance auf ein Leben, das nirgendwo sonst auf der Welt aufregender und vielseitiger sein könnte.

Es ist schwierig, einen typischen New Yorker zu beschreiben, aber noch schwieriger ist es, ein typisches New Yorker Heim zu beschreiben – außer dass es vielleicht gewagt, originell und auf keinen Fall vorhersehbar ist. Die Liebe der New Yorker zur Kultur und ihre Leidenschaft für Kunst lässt sich gleichermaßen gut in umgebauten Lofts, modernistischen Penthouses oder traditionellen Stadthäusern zeigen. Außerdem befindet sich die Stadt im ständigen Fluss: Viertel entwickeln sich und richten sich innerhalb weniger Jahre neu aus. Seit ich in New York lebe, hat sich Chelsea zum Beispiel von einem spärlich bewohnten kunstfixierten Außenposten in ein beliebtes Viertel für Familien verwandelt und das nur, weil eine neue Schule hinzugekommen ist. Oder nehmen wir den Meatpacking District – dessen Erscheinungsbild einst Schlachter und Lieferwagen prägten –, in dem sich heute der viel beachtete High Line Park befindet und der Chelsea Market mit seinem wunderbar geschäftigen Treiben. Oder Brooklyn, das ein scheinbar endloses Spektrum an neuen Restaurants, kulturellen Veranstaltungen, Künstlern und talentierten Möbelherstellern bietet.

Anders als in vielen europäischen Städten, in denen ich gelebt habe, lassen die New Yorker ihren Designideen freien Lauf. Es gibt keine übliche Norm, an die man sich halten muss, oder Regeln, die bestimmen, „wie etwas zu sein hat". Ich finde diese Freiheit sowohl erfrischend als auch herausfordernd. New Yorker schrecken in ihren Wohnräumen nicht vor Farbe zurück. Und sie sind unglaublich erfinderisch, was die Architektur und das Finden von Lösungen betrifft, um klassische New Yorker Elemente in neue Kontexte zu setzen – wie zum Beispiel eine gusseiserne Säule, um die sich ein Sitzelement gruppiert. Aber damit nicht genug, sie haben auch keine Angst davor, das ganze Konzept eines urbanen Dschungels neu zu definieren, indem sie die Innen- und Außenwände ihrer Häuser bepflanzen.

Ich lebe seit fünfzehn Jahren hier und erfahre gerade am eigenen Leib, wie grenzenlos die Auswahl und groß das Talent bei der Gestaltung von Innenräumen ist, da ich mein Zuhause renovieren lasse. Während ich an vielen anderen Orten ein Schema hatte, an das ich mich halten konnte, bin ich hier auf mich allein gestellt. Es ist aufregend (und auch ein bisschen beängstigend) zu entscheiden, wer man ist und wie die eigene Welt aussehen soll. Aber geht es in New York nicht genau darum, um diese Bereitschaft, etwas Besonderes schaffen zu wollen? Man kommt an, beschließt, wer man sein möchte, und geht dann hinaus und gibt sein Bestes, um es zu werden – und tut dies so häufig, wie man es möchte.

Introduction
Vanessa Weiner von Bismarck

BIEN PEU DE villes de la planète sont aussi diversifiées que New York et donc rien d'étonnant à ce que les demeures là-bas présentent une gamme exceptionnelle de différents styles. Un incroyable mélange de personnes venues de divers pays et pour qui cette ville extraordinaire est leur port d'attache signifie qu'un élément de surprise est un phénomène constant. Véritable aimant pour des personnes créatives et dynamiques dans tous les secteurs, ses rues et ses locaux sont superchargés d'une énergie éclectique. Pour tous ceux qui y vivent (que ce soit les résidents de longue date ou les nouveaux venus au regard émerveillé), New York offre aux gens la chance de se créer une vie qui sera trépidante et variée comme nulle part ailleurs.

Tout comme il est difficile de définir un New Yorkais typique, il est encore plus ardu de définir un espace typique de New York, à moins de dire qu'il sera probablement plein d'audace, original et certainement imprévisible. L'affection des New Yorkais pour la culture et leur passion pour l'art transparaissent tout autant dans les lofts industriels convertis, les penthouses modernistes ou les maisons de ville traditionnelles. De plus la ville est en transformation constante. Les quartiers évoluent et se reconfigurent en l'espace d'un très petit nombre d'années. Pour donner un exemple, depuis que je suis arrivée à New York, Chelsea qui était un bastion à orientation artistique et peu peuplé, s'est métamorphosé en un des quartiers à vocation familiale parmi les plus recherchés simplement en se dotant d'une nouvelle école. Ou bien prenez le Meatpacking District qui fut le fief des bouchers et des camions de livraison et où vous trouvez aujourd'hui le High Line dont on parle tellement et le Chelsea Market si merveilleusement animé. Ou Brooklyn qui offre une gamme infinie de nouveaux restaurants, événements culturels, artistes et fabricants de meubles talentueux.

À la différence des nombreuses villes européennes où j'ai vécu, les New Yorkais laissent libre cours à leur imagination créatrice. Il n'existe pas de normes conventionnelles à suivre ou des règles pour définir ce qui « doit se faire ». Je trouve que cette liberté est à la fois un bol d'air et un défi. Les New Yorkais ne sont pas intimidés par les couleurs dans leur espace de vie. Ils sont aussi incroyablement astucieux quand il s'agit d'architecture ou pour trouver un moyen de réinventer les éléments classiques de New York, comme par exemple transformer une colonne de fer forgé en une magnifique pièce de centre pour un banc. Et si ça ne suffit pas, ils n'ont pas peur de redéfinir tout le concept de jungle urbaine en cultivant des jardins sur les murs intérieurs et extérieurs.

Ayant vécu ici pendant quinze ans et passant maintenant moi aussi par une phase de complet renouveau, j'ai appris par expérience propre que s'agissant d'intérieurs, les choix sont vraiment infinis et que les talents abondent. Alors que dans beaucoup d'autres endroits je devais suivre un modèle, ici je suis livrée à moi-même. C'est grisant (et aussi un petit chouïa terrifiant) de pouvoir choisir qui vous êtes et à quoi doit ressembler votre univers. Et pourtant, n'est pas ce désir de créer quelque chose d'extraordinaire qui est vraiment l'esprit de New York ? Vous arrivez ici, vous décidez qui vous voulez être et puis vous êtes partis et vous faites de votre mieux pour le devenir autant de fois et aussi souvent que vous le voulez.

Party Pad
Chelsea

PERCHED ON A corner of a high-rise designed by architect Annabelle Selldorf in Chelsea, designer Jamie Drake's 3,000-square-foot condo boasts 16-foot-tall ceilings, sweeping views, and an elevator that lifts his Rolls-Royce to its own parking spot. Its wide-open areas are also ideal for hosting massive parties, which Drake often throws. "I love to entertain," he says. He saw the environs as an opportunity for a "fresh start" and took a new track with his interior design. Never hesitant to explore uncharted design turf, Drake defined the rooms with ebonized teak floors and walls in shades of gray. And after selling most of his old furnishings, he brought in a virtually whole new set of pieces, he says, adding that he only kept "my 1960s *Hand* chair by Pedro Friedeberg, a Chuck Close painting, and a few sentimental items."

DIE 280 QUADRATMETER große Eigentumswohnung des Innenarchitekten Jamie Drake liegt auf einer Ecke des von der Architektin Annabelle Selldorf entworfenen Hochhauses in Chelsea. Sie zeichnet sich durch 5 Meter hohe Decken, weite Ausblicke und einen Aufzug aus, der dessen Rolls-Royce zu seiner eigenen Garage befördert. Die offenen Wohnräume eignen sich ebenfalls bestens, um große Partys zu geben, was bei Drake häufig vorkommt. „Ich liebe es, Gäste zu bewirten", erklärt er. Er betrachtete die Umgebung auch als Möglichkeit, in seiner Innenarchitektur in unerforschte Gebiete vorzudringen. So stattete Drake die neuen Räume mit ebenierten Teakböden und -wänden in Grautönen aus. Nachdem er fast sein gesamtes altes Mobiliar verkauft hatte, und nur, wie er sagt, „meinen ‚Hand'-Stuhl von Pedro Friedeberg aus den 1960er-Jahren, ein Gemälde von Chuck Close und ein paar Erinnerungsstücke" behielt, richtete er sich quasi völlig neu ein.

PERCHÉ AU COIN d'un gratte-ciel conçu par l'architecte Annabelle Selldorf à Chelsea, l'appartement de près de 280 mètres carrés du décorateur Jamie Drake présente des plafonds de plus de 5 mètres, des vues panoramiques et un ascenseur qui monte sa Rolls-Royce jusqu'à sa place de parking privé. Ses grands espaces ouverts sont idéals pour organiser des parties géantes ce dont Drake ne se prive pas. « J'aime recevoir », nous dit-il. Il percevait les environs comme l'occasion d'un « nouveau départ » et il décida d'un changement de direction dans sa décoration d'intérieurs. N'hésitant jamais à explorer de nouveaux territoires dans la décoration, Drake définit les pièces avec des planchers en tek ébène et des murs dans des tons de gris. Et après avoir vendu la majeure partie de ses anciens meubles, il nous explique qu'il fit venir un ensemble complet de nouvelles pièces, en ajoutant qu'il a gardé uniquement « mon siège 'main' de Pedro Friedeberg, datant de 1960, un tableau de Chuck Close et des objets à caractère sentimental ».

Foregoing a dining table altogether, designer Jamie Drake created multiple seating zones with low tables that support his casual style of entertaining.

Innenarchitekt Jamie Drake verzichtete gänzlich auf einen Esstisch und schuf mehrere Sitzmöglichkeiten mit tiefen Tischen, die seinem lockeren Stil der Bewirtung von Gästen entgegenkommen.

Le décorateur Jamie Drake a laissé de côté le concept de grande table pour créer de multiples zones avec des sièges et des petites tables basses, en accord avec son style décontracté pour recevoir.

The open kitchen's two-tiered island features a gold-leafed cabinet and a white Corian counter that overlaps at a dramatic angle.

Die zweiteilige Insel in der offenen Küche zeichnet sich durch einen vergoldeten Kabinettschrank und eine weiße Corian-Arbeitsplatte aus, die in einem dramatischen Winkel darüber liegt.

L'îlot à deux niveaux de la cuisine ouverte présente une armoire dorée à la feuille et un plan de travail en corian blanc qui se superposent en formant un angle spectaculaire.

Gray lacquer walls cloak the master bedroom with a sexy air. The bath features walls with a peachy Venetian plaster.

Graue Lackwände verleihen dem großen Schlafzimmer eine sexy Atmosphäre. Das Bad wird durch die Wände aus venezianischem Putz bestimmt.

Des murs laqués gris donnent un air sexy à la chambre principale. La salle de bains présente des murs de stuc vénitien couleur pêche.

When Drake hosts extra-large parties, the designer parks his car outside and uses the garage to complement the outdoor lounge space.

Wenn Drake sehr große Partys gibt, parkt der Innenarchitekt seinen Wagen draußen und nutzt die Garage als Extrafläche.

Lorsque Drake organise des parties super géantes, le décorateur stationne sa voiture dehors et utilise son garage en prolongement du salon extérieur.

Urban Oasis
Gramercy

UPON ENTERING THIS 4,600-square-foot duplex, one is instantly enveloped with a sense of serenity—rare in the city that never sleeps. Located in a minimalist building, the double-height space offers appealing views of Union Square. The owners' primary goal was the option to turn off the city's hustle and bustle and escape into an inner sanctum. Working with a rich mix of materials—steel, marble, leather, horsehair, and various woods—interior designer Dominic Gasparoly and architect Khalid Watson of the New York/Los Angeles–based studio GWdesign warmed up the cool shell and transformed the residence into an urban oasis. The centerpiece is a gravity-defying wooden staircase that almost appears to float within the dramatic foyer. Beyond the entrance are quieter spaces, including the living room and a lounge with a fireplace and dry bar. A terrace features a vertical garden complete with its own fountain and reflection pool.

SOBALD MAN DIESE 430 Quadratmeter große doppelgeschossige Wohnung betritt, wird man umhüllt von Gelassenheit – etwas Seltenes in der Stadt, die niemals schläft. Die sich in einem minimalistischen Gebäude befindenden Räume bieten reizvolle Blicke auf den Union Square. Vorrangiges Ziel war es, die Hektik der Stadt hinter sich zu lassen und an einen Ort zurückzuziehen, an dem man sich besinnen kann. Der Innenarchitekt Dominic Gasparoly und der Architekt Khalid Watson von dem in New York und Los Angeles beheimateten Büro GWdesign arbeiteten mit einer Fülle von Materialien – Stahl, Marmor, Leder, Rosshaar und verschiedenen Hölzern. Sie wärmten die kühle äußere Schale auf und verwandelten das Wohnhaus in eine Oase in der Stadt. Herzstück des Hauses ist eine der Schwerkraft trotzende Holztreppe, die in der dramatischen Eingangshalle fast zu schweben scheint. Dahinter befinden sich ruhigere Räume, unter anderem das Wohnzimmer und eine Lounge mit Kamin und Bar. Die Terrasse endet in einem fantastischen vertikalen Garten mitsamt Brunnen und Reflexionsbecken.

AU MOMENT D'ENTRER dans ce duplex de près de 430 mètre carrés, vous ressentez immédiatement un sentiment de sérénité ce qui est rare dans la ville qui ne dort jamais. Situé dans un bâtiment aux lignes minimalistes, cet espace à double hauteur offre des vues captivantes sur Union Square. Le principal objectif des propriétaires était de s'échapper de la vie trépidante de la ville pour trouver refuge dans un sanctuaire propice à la réflexion. Le décorateur d'intérieur Dominic Gasparoly et l'architecte Khalid Watson du studio GWdesign basé à New York et Los Angeles ont utilisé un riche mélange de matériaux comme l'acier, le marbre, le cuir, le crin de cheval et plusieurs bois pour donner une atmosphère chaleureuse à ces lignes épurées et transformer cette résidence en une oasis urbaine. L'élément central est un escalier en bois défiant les lois de la gravité qui semble pratiquement flotter dans une entrée féérique. Au premier niveau se trouvent les espaces les plus tranquilles, un salon et un boudoir orné d'une cheminée et d'un bar sec. Une terrasse se présente comme un jardin vertical complet avec sa propre fontaine et un miroir d'eau.

A custom chandelier (previous page) and staircase pull together the two levels of this airy duplex.

Ein nach den Wünschen des Kunden gefertigter Kronleuchter (vorige Seite) und eine Treppe verbinden die beiden Ebenen dieses luftigen Doppelgeschossapartments.

Un lustre fait sur mesure (page précédente) et un escalier réunissent les deux niveaux de ce duplex aéré.

Most of the furnishings and even some accents, including the teak and metal table in the dining area and the cutting board in the open kitchen, were custom-designed by GWdesign. The master bedroom's ceiling is covered with whitewashed oak.

Der größte Teil der Einrichtung und selbst einige der gesetzten Akzente, wie der Teak- und Metalltisch im Essbereich und das Schneidebrett in der offenen Küche, wurden von GWdesign entworfen. Die Decke des großen Schlafzimmers wurde mit gebleichtem Eichenholz verkleidet.

La plupart du mobilier et même certains éléments décoratifs comme la table en tek et métal de l'espace repas et le plan de travail dans la cuisine ouverte ont été faits sur mesure par GWdesign. Le plafond de la chambre principale est recouvert de chêne blanchi.

Floating vanities keep the baths feeling airy and light while stained white oak drawers and shelves add warmth.

Schwebende Waschtische lassen die Bäder luftig und leicht erscheinen, während Eichenschubladen und -regale ihnen Wärme verleihen.

Des armoires de rangement détachées donnent un air léger et aéré aux salles de bains et les tiroirs et les étagères en bois de chêne blanchi ajoutent une touche chaleureuse.

Adjacent to the lounge, a terrace stretches the duplex's entire width and culminates with a vertical garden, fountain, and reflection pool.

An die Lounge angrenzend erstreckt sich über die gesamte Breite des Apartments eine Terrasse, die in einem vertikalen Garten mit Brunnen und Reflexionsbecken gipfelt.

Une terrasse filante, adjacente au boudoir, s'étire sur toute la longueur du duplex et mène à un jardin vertical avec fontaine et miroir d'eau.

Simply Redd
Nolita

KNOWN FOR HIS brash streak, decorator Miles Redd made the most of a taste for tension in his 1826 townhouse in Nolita, a neighborhood north of Little Italy. Like the fantasies he conjures to find design inspiration, he riffed on the concept of "Hollywood's interpretation of 1930s New York" and added "a dash of Parisian savoir faire." Using the 3,900-square-foot townhouse as a laboratory for his ideas, he deployed an eclectic mix of materials, furnishings, and art to generate layers of contrast—"high and low, glossy next to crumbling, modern next to antique." The home's tour de force is a mirrored bathroom, originally designed by the American architect David Adler in 1930 for a larger house and reinstalled in Redd's master suite. Dovetailing its elements into the smaller space "had its challenges," says the decorator. "But we just pushed forward."

DER FÜR SEINE schrille Ader bekannte Raumgestalter Miles Redd kostete seine Vorliebe für Spannung bei seinem 1826 gebauten Stadthaus in Nolita, einem Viertel nördlich von Little Italy, im höchsten Maße aus. So wie in seinen Fantasien, die er heraufbeschwört, um seine Designinspirationen zu finden, variierte er die Vorstellung von „Hollywoods Interpretation des New Yorks der 1930er-Jahre", und fügte noch etwas „Pariser Savoir-faire" hinzu. Er nutzte sein 360 Quadratmeter großes Stadthaus als Labor für seine Ideen und setzte eine vielseitige Mischung aus Materialien, Möbeln und Kunst ein, um Spannungen zu erzeugen – „Bedeutendes und Gewöhnliches, Glattes neben Zerfallendem, Modernes neben Antikem." Das Meisterstück des Hauses ist das verspiegelte Badezimmer, das von dem amerikanischen Architekten David Adler ursprünglich für ein größeres Haus entworfen und in Redds Mastersuite eingebaut wurde. Die Einzelteile auf den kleineren Raum anzupassen „stellte uns vor Herausforderungen", so der Raumgestalter. „Aber wir haben sie einfach hineingezwängt."

CONNU POUR SON style provocateur, le décorateur Miles Redd a su tirer parti de son goût pour les contradictions dans sa maison de ville de 1826 à Nolita, un quartier au nord de la Petite Italie. Tout comme les fantaisies qu'il évoque pour trouver de l'inspiration pour son décor, il a fait appel au concept de « l'interprétation d'Hollywood de New York des années 1930 » et a ajouté « une pincée de savoir-faire parisien ». Il a transformé cette maison de ville de près de 360 mètres carrés en laboratoire pour ses idées en y déployant un brassage éclectique de matériaux, mobilier et objets d'art pour créer des superpositions tout en contraste : « haut et bas, rutilant allié au décrépit, moderne à côté d'une antiquité ». La pièce tour de force est la salle de bains à miroirs conçue à l'origine par l'architecte américain, David Adler, en 1930 pour une maison plus grande et réinstallée dans la suite principale. L'intégration des éléments dans un espace plus petit « fut un défi à relever », nous dit le décorateur. « Mais nous nous sommes attelés à la tâche. »

A Hollywood take on 1930s New York with a Parisian tinge inspired the decor in Miles Redd's townhouse.

Hollywoods Bild des New Yorks der 1930er-Jahre und ein Hauch von Paris inspirierten Miles Redd bei der Ausstattung seines Hauses.

Une interprétation d'Hollywood des années 1930 à New York avec une touche parisienne ont inspiré le décor de la maison de ville de Miles Redd.

The master suite, including a canopied bed and a mirrored bath, gushes with glamour.

Die Mastersuite mitsamt Himmelbett und verspiegeltem Badezimmer quillt über vor Glamour.

La suite principale comprenant un lit à baldaquins et une salle de bains à miroirs est une explosion de glamour.

Accent on Art
TriBeCa

LOCATED IN A former warehouse in TriBeCa, this loft's owner is an art aficionado. When he found the 2,300-square-foot space, he knew its high ceilings and open plan would afford the perfect backdrop for his collection. To make it viable for his lifestyle, architect Dirk Denison gutted the top-floor and worked with designer Sara Story to create fresh interiors. Leaving a few brick walls exposed, the duo kept the loft feeling airy with oak floors and plaster walls throughout. To create an energetic atmosphere, the designer introduced a mix of new and mid-century pieces, including a Pierre Chareau fan table and a vintage "belt" leather rug. "Each piece has its own interesting story—something I found in Buenos Aires or on a trip to Paris," says the designer.

DER BESITZER DIESES Lofts in einem früheren Lagerhaus in TriBeCa ist ein Kunstliebhaber. Als er den 210 Quadratmeter großen Raum fand, wusste er, dass die hohen Decken und die offene Raumstruktur eine perfekte Umgebung für seine Sammlung bilden würden. Um das Loft dem Lebensstil des Besitzers anzupassen, ließ der Architekt Dirk Denison das obere Stockwerk entkernen und arbeitete mit der Innenarchitektin Sara Story zusammen, um frische Innenräume zu schaffen. Das Duo behielt den luftigen Eindruck des Lofts bei, indem sie Eichenholzböden verlegten und die Wände verputzten – bis auf wenige Ausnahmen, an denen die Ziegelsteine sichtbar blieben. Um eine dynamische Atmosphäre zu schaffen, wählte die Innenarchitektin eine Mischung aus neuen und aus der Mitte des vergangenen Jahrhunderts stammenden Einrichtungsgegenständen, darunter auch ein Fächertisch von Pierre Chareau und ein Streifenteppich aus Leder. „Sämtliche Stücke haben ihre eigene Geschichte – einige fand ich in Buenos Aires, andere auf einer Reise nach Paris", sagt die Innenarchitektin.

LE PROPRIÉTAIRE DE ce loft situé dans un ancien entrepôt de TriBeCa est un grand amateur d'art. Lorsqu'il découvrit cet espace de près de 210 mètres carrés, il sut immédiatement que les hauts plafonds et la conception ouverte allait lui apporter le cadre parfait pour sa collection. Pour le rendre conforme à son style de vie, l'architecte Dirk Denison a complètement démoli le niveau du haut et a travaillé avec la décoratrice Sara Story pour créer des intérieurs rafraichissants. Le duo laissa quelques murs en brique apparents et garda l'aspect aéré du loft avec des planchers en chêne et des murs de stuc tout autour. Pour créer une atmosphère dynamique, la décoratrice a ajouté un mélange de pièces modernes datant des années 1950 dont une table avec hotte de Pierre Chareau et un tapis vintage fait avec des « ceintures » de cuir. « Chaque pièce a une histoire à raconter, ce sont des choses que j'ai déniché à Buenos Aires ou lors d'un voyage à Paris », nous dit la décoratrice.

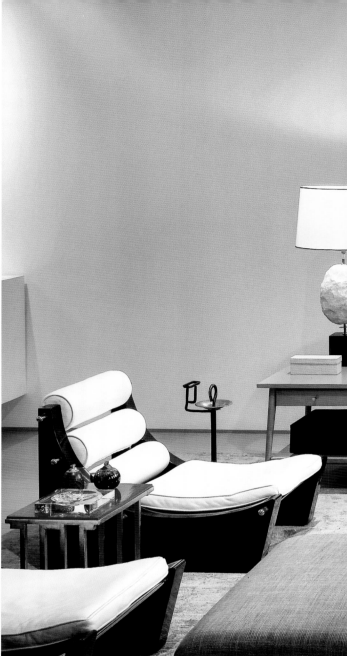

A backdrop of neutral furnishings and materials in black, white, brown, and beige allow art to stand out. The white stone composite kitchen counters reflect light from oversize pendants.

In einer Umgebung neutraler Möbel und Materialien in Schwarz, Weiß, Braun und Beige kann die Kunst hervortreten. Die Küchentheken aus weißem Kunststein reflektieren das Licht übergroßer Hängelampen.

Un arrière-plan de mobilier neutre et de matériaux en noir, blanc, marron et beige font ressortir les œuvres d'art. Les plans de travail de la cuisine en pierre blanche composite reflètent la lumière des luminaires géants pendus au plafond.

The colors of a painted bench allude to those in the painting by Trey Speegle over the sectional in the den/guest room. An office niche hides behind a custom rolling zinc door.

Eine bemalte Bank im Arbeits- und Gästezimmer verweist auf die Farben in dem über der Couchgarnitur hängenden Bild von Trey Speegle. Die Büronische verbirgt sich hinter eigens angefertigten Schiebetüren aus Zink.

Les couleurs du banc peint reprennent celles du tableau de Trey Speegle au-dessus du canapé d'angle du petit salon/ chambre d'ami. Un bureau se dissimule derrière une porte coulissante en zinc faite sur mesure.

The architect removed one bedroom to create an expansive master suite. Italian luce di luna *marble defines the master bath.*

Der Architekt entfernte ein Schlafzimmer, um eine große Mastersuite zu schaffen. Luce-di-luna-Marmor zeichnet das dazugehörige Bad aus.

L'architecte a supprimé une chambre pour créer une immense chambre principale. Le marbre italien luce di luna *définit la salle de bains principale.*

Uptown Chic
Carnegie Hill

AS NATIVE NEW Yorkers, this Park Avenue co-op's owners were completely at ease with its Carnegie Hill neighborhood yet wanted to steer clear of stereotypical "old-school" decor by cultivating fresh environs for their young family. "My clients definitely didn't want their home looking 'preppy,'" says designer Katie Ridder, who created the interiors. "It's a young person's apartment, so they wanted it to be pared down and reflect who they were." Working with architect John Murray, they gutted the 2,800-square-foot, four-bedroom space and gave it new life with quality millwork and moldings. They then paired these features with a lively palette and custom and vintage furnishings. "The overall style is classical, but it's zippy with personality and flair." Though the owners originally wanted to keep the spaces neutral, color eventually crept in. "At the end of the day," notes Ridder, "spaces without color just aren't as interesting"—as these uplifting rooms prove.

ALS GEBÜRTIGE NEW Yorker gingen die Besitzer dieses Apartments auf der Park Avenue ganz gelassen mit ihrer Carnegie-Hill-Umgebung um, wollten sich aber von der stereotypen, althergebrachten Einrichtungsweise eindeutig abheben und ihr für ihre junge Familie eine frische Note verliehen. „Meine Kunden wollten auf keinen Fall ein ,adrett' aussehendes Zuhause", sagt die Interiordesignerin Katie Ridder, die die Innenräume schuf. „Das Apartment gehört jungen Leuten. Es sollte reduzierter sein und ihre Persönlichkeit widerspiegeln." Zusammen mit dem Architekten John Murray entkernte sie die 260 Quadratmeter große, vier Schlafzimmer umfassende Wohnung und hauchte ihr mit einem hochwertigen Innenausbau neues Leben ein. Dann versah sie diese Ausstattung mit einer lebendigen Farbpalette und richtete die Wohnung mit sowohl eigens angefertigten als auch Vintage-Stücken ein. „Der Stil insgesamt ist zwar klassisch, wirkt aber durch die persönliche Note und den Flair frisch." Obwohl die Besitzer die Räume ursprünglich neutral gestaltet haben wollten, schlich sich zum Schluss doch Farbe hinein. „Letztendlich", bemerkt Ridder, „sind Räume ohne Farbe einfach nicht so interessant" – wie diese schwungvollen Zimmer beweisen.

EN TANT QUE vrais New Yorkais d'origine, les propriétaires de cet appartement coopératif sur la Park Avenue se sentaient complètement à l'aise dans le quartier de Carnegie Hill mais ils voulaient éviter le décor stéréotypé de la « vieille école » et développer un environnement inédit pour leur jeune famille. « Mes clients ne voulaient surtout pas que leur demeure ait un air BCBG », nous dit la décoratrice Katie Ridder, qui a créé les intérieurs. « C'est un appartement jeune et donc ils ne le voulaient pas trop surchargé tout en reflétant leur personnalité. » Ensemble avec l'architecte John Murray, ils ont complètement démoli cet espace de près de 260 mètres carrés et quatre chambres et lui ont donné un nouveau souffle de vie avec de la menuiserie et des moulures de qualité. Puis ils ont ajouté une palette de couleurs vives et des meubles faits sur mesure et vintage. « Dans l'ensemble, il s'agit d'un style classique mais il est pimenté de personnalité et d'originalité. » Bien qu'à l'origine les propriétaires voulaient conserver des tons neutres pour les espaces, la couleur finit par s'imposer. « Au bout du compte », note Katie Ridder, « les espaces sans couleurs ne sont pas tellement intéressants », comme le prouve ces pièces qui vous remontent le moral.

The home's color scheme began in the dining room, with its turquoise blue walls. Red accents and a palette also including shades of olive, orange, and brown carry through to other rooms.

Ausgangspunkt für die Farbgebung der Wohnung waren die türkisfarbenen Wände im Esszimmer. Rote Farbakzente und eine Palette, die Oliv-, Orange- und Brauntöne beinhaltet, durchziehen die anderen Räume.

Le thème des couleurs de cette maison commence dans la salle à manger avec ses murs bleu turquoise. Des touches de rouge et une palette comprenant des tons vert olive, orange et marron se retrouvent dans d'autres pièces.

Modern Sophistication
Central Park West

RARELY DOES A designer receive carte blanche to design a home in New York. But such was the stroke of luck bestowed upon designer John Willey, when a couple asked him to design their 3,800-square-foot, five-bedroom pied-à-terre at 15 Central Park West—where all of the apartment's rooms overlook Central Park. Because of the magnificent views, says Willey, "nature was my inspiration." Amid a palette of pale blue, beige, terra cotta, sage, chocolate brown, and silver, and a trove of vintage furnishings—such as a circa 1950 buffet by Paul László, a 1940s oak console by Paul T. Frankl, and a console of Macassar ebony with silver-painted rope by Christian Astuguevieille—presents an air of relaxed glamour. To keep the ambience fresh, the designer paired refined pieces, like a vintage high-gloss dresser, with more humble ones, like woven rope beds. "It takes the seriousness out of the equation," notes Willey, "but keeps it sophisticated."

SELTEN WIRD EINEM Innenarchitekten freie Hand bei der Gestaltung einer Wohnung in New York gelassen, doch dieses Glück war John Willey beschieden, als ein Paar ihn bat, seine 350 Quadratmeter große, fünf Schlafzimmer umfassende Zweitwohnung am Central Park West 15 zu gestalten, deren sämtliche Räume über einen Blick auf den Central Park verfügen. „Aufgrund der wunderbaren Aussicht", sagt Willey, „war die Natur Quelle meiner Inspiration". In einer Farbpalette von Blassblau, Beige, Terrakotta, Graugrün, Schokoladenbraun und Silber bietet ein Schatz von Vintage-Möbeln – darunter ein um 1950 geschaffenes Büffet von Paul Lázló, eine Eichenkonsole aus den 1940er-Jahren von Paul T. Frankl und eine Konsole aus Makassar-Ebenholz mit einem silbern bemalten Seil von Christian Astuguevieille – eine Atmosphäre entspannten Glamours. Um das Ambiente lebendig zu halten, kombinierte der Innenarchitekt erlesene Möbel – wie zum Beispiel eine alte Hochglanzkommode – mit einfacheren Stücken wie Betten aus geflochtenen Seilen. „So wird aus der Gleichung die Ernsthaftigkeit genommen", merkt Willey an, „ohne dass die Raffinesse darunter leidet".

IL EST RARE qu'un décorateur reçoive carte blanche pour aménager une résidence à New York mais ce fut le coup de chance du décorateur John Willey lorsqu'un couple lui demanda de refaire complètement leur pied à terre de près de 350 mètres carrés et cinq chambres au 15 Central Park West, avec toutes les pièces de l'appartement donnant sur Central Park. En raison de la vue magnifique nous dit Willey, « la nature fut mon inspiration ». Une palette de bleu clair, beige, terra cotta, vert sauge, chocolat et argent alliée à un trésor de meubles vintage comme un buffet 1950 de Paul László, une console des années 1940 en chêne de Paul T. Frankl et une console en ébène de Macassar avec une corde peinte en argent de Christian Astuguevieille apportent un air glamour décontracté. Pour que l'ambiance garde sa fraicheur, le décorateur a associé des éléments raffinés comme une armoire vintage laquée brillante avec d'autres plus humbles comme des lits en corde tressée. « Voilà ce qui nous enlève le sérieux de l'équation, tout en gardant un ton élégant », nous fait remarquer Willey.

Closets in a hall were removed to make room for a reading niche surrounded by grass-covered cloth walls. A bath was painted sage green for pop.

In einer Diele wurden Schränke entfernt, um eine mit Grastapeten geschmückte Leseecke zu schaffen. Ein Bad wurde in einem lebendigen Graugrün gestrichen.

Les placards dans le couloir furent remplacés par un coin lecture agrémenté de tissu vert pré. La salle de bains fut peinte en vert sauge pour faire ressortir la couleur.

A walnut and vellum nightstand by Mattaliano flanks a bed in one of the bedrooms. The floors and walls of the master bath are lined in Calacatta Gold marble.

In einem der Schlafzimmer steht neben einem Bett ein Nachttisch aus Walnussholz und Velin von Mattaliano. Die Böden und Wände im Masterbad sind mit Calacatta-Gold-Marmor verkleidet.

Une table de nuit en noyer et vélin de Mattaliano se trouve à côté du lit dans une des chambres. Le sol et les murs de la salle de bains principale sont revêtus de marbre doré de Calacatta.

The upholstery and rugs in most rooms were custom-designed by the designer's studio.

Die meisten Polstermöbel und Teppiche in den Räumen wurden im Atelier des Innenarchitekten maßgefertigt.

Dans la plupart des pièces, les revêtements en tissu et les tapis furent faits sur mesure dans le studio du décorateur.

Color Story
NoHo

UPGRADING FROM A bohemian space in TriBeCa, the young photographer living in this condo loft near Astor Place wanted to preserve the arty atmosphere but also desired a stronger sense of style. "She didn't want it overly 'decorated,' but she likes color—and she loves to entertain," says interior designer Christopher Coleman. With a nod of approval on a vibrant palette and a mandate to create a variety of gathering spaces, Coleman crafted a playful yet comfortable home with a rich mix of bright furnishings and industrial elements that echo the building's former life as a manufacturing facility. A hot pink sofa by Vladimir Kagan accented with a pair of suspended cocoon chairs set the living area's spirited tone. And a mélange of other pieces—from the patterned dining room chairs to the factory stools at the kitchen island—extends the casual whimsy "to all the other nooks and crannies where people congregate."

DIE JUNGE FOTOGRAFIN, die vorher in unkonventionellen Räumen in TriBeCa wohnte und sich mit dem Kauf dieses Lofts, das sich in der Nähe des Astor Place befindet, wohnlich verbesserte, wollte die künstlerische Atmosphäre beibehalten, trotzdem aber stilvoller leben. „Sie wollte die Wohnung nicht übermäßig ‚dekoriert' haben, doch mag sie Farben und liebt es, Gäste zu bewirten", erklärt der Innenarchitekt Christopher Coleman. Nachdem eine lebendige Farbpalette ihren Zuspruch fand und Coleman den Auftrag erhielt, eine Reihe von Sitzecken zu schaffen, richtete er die Wohnung mit einer Mischung aus leuchtenden Möbeln und Industrieelementen ein, die das frühere Leben des Gebäudes als Produktionsstätte aufnehmen. Ein prächtiges pinkfarbenes Sofa von Vladimir Kagan und zwei Hängesessel geben in dem lebendig wirkenden Wohnbereich den Ton an. Eine Kombination unterschiedlicher Einrichtungsgegenstände – von den gemusterten Esszimmerstühlen bis hin zu den Industriehockern in der Küche – setzt die lockere Atmosphäre „in allen Ecken und Winkeln, in denen Menschen zusammenkommen" fort.

POUR LA JEUNE photographe qui a emménagé dans ce loft en copropriété près d'Astor Place ce fut une amélioration par rapport à son espace bohême dans TriBeCa. Elle a voulu préserver son atmosphère artistique tout en souhaitant y ajouter beaucoup plus de style. « Elle ne voulait pas qu'il soit exagérément 'décoré', mais elle aime les couleurs et elle adore recevoir », nous explique le décorateur d'intérieur, Christopher Coleman. Après un signe d'approbation pour une palette haute en couleurs et la mission de créer de multiples espaces de réunion, Coleman a produit une demeure ludique mais confortable avec un mélange chatoyant de meubles de couleurs vives et d'éléments industriels pour rappeler le passé du bâtiment qui était une ancienne usine désaffectée. Un canapé rose vif de Vladimir Kagan accentué par une paire de fauteuils cocon suspendus donne un ton de gaité au séjour. Un mélange d'autres pièces, des chaises de la salle à manger avec des motifs aux tabourets d'usine de l'îlot de cuisine, apportent ce romantisme décontracté « à tous les autres coins et recoins où les personnes se réunissent ».

Curvy furnishings upholstered in shades of hot pink, lemon yellow, turquoise, and avocado pep up the former industrial space with organic shapes and jolts of color.

Geschwungene Polstermöbel in leuchtenden Pink-, Zitronengelb-, Türkis- und Avocadotönen bringen mit ihren organischen Formen und ihrer Farbigkeit Schwung in den ehemals gewerblich genutzten Raum.

Des meubles arrondis tapissés dans des tons rose vif, jaune citron, turquoise et avocat pimentent l'ancien espace industriel avec des formes bio et des jets de couleur.

Handles made of leather and antique brass contrast with the avocado green-stained wood cabinets in the kitchen.

Griffe aus Leder und antikem Messing heben sich von den avocadogrün gebeizten Holzschränken in der Küche ab.

Des poignées faites de cuir et laiton patiné contrastent avec les armoires de bois de la cuisine de teinte vert avocat.

Covered with turquoise mosaic tiles, every wall of the master bath was designed for impact.

Die mit türkisfarbenen Mosaiksteinen gefliesten Wände im Badezimmer wurden alle effektvoll gestaltet.

Couverts de carreaux en mosaïque turquoise, tous les murs de la salle de bains principale ont été conçus pour faire de l'effet.

Comfort Zone
Southampton

SHORTLY AFTER THIS shingle-style retreat's globetrotting owner acquired the house in Southampton, he purchased some adjoining farmland, reconfigured the lots, rebuilt the 6,850-square-foot main house, and later constructed a 5,500-square-foot guesthouse next door. After working with the late Connecticut-based architect Richard Sawicki to design the houses, he undertook the process of furnishing the interiors himself. "To me, my environment is a personal thing and I want to be comfortable in it," says the owner. And so, with comfort as the underlying driver for the decor, he gradually filled the rooms of both houses with classic furnishings and French and English antiques he picked during his travels. The soothing neutral palette and mostly traditional furniture are spiced with brightly colored accents and art, including an array of paintings by Stefan Szczesny. "I saw an exhibition of his work in London and called the artist the next day and bought the whole set."

KURZ NACHDEM DER um die Welt reisende Eigentümer diesen im Schindelstil gebauten Rückzugsort in Southampton erwarb, kaufte er auch das benachbarte Grundstück, gestaltete beide um und ließ zuerst das 640 Quadratmeter große Haupthaus um- und später ein 510 Quadratmeter großes Gästehaus nebenan erbauen. Für den Entwurf der Häuser beauftragte er den in Connecticut lebenden, kürzlich verstorbenen Architekten Richard Sawicki und richtete dann die Innenräume selbst ein. „Die Umgebung, in der ich lebe, ist für mich etwas Persönliches, und ich möchte mich darin wohlfühlen", erklärt der Besitzer. Diesem Leitmotiv der Behaglichkeit folgend, stattete er beide Häuser nach und nach mit klassischen Möbeln und französischen und englischen Antiquitäten aus, die er von seinen Reisen mitbrachte. Die beruhigend neutrale Farbpalette und das zumeist traditionelle Mobiliar werden durch farbenfrohe Akzente und Kunst aufgelockert, unter der sich auch eine Reihe von Bildern von Stefan Szczesny befindet. „Ich sah eine Ausstellung seiner Werke in London und rief ihn am nächsten Tag an, um die ganze Serie davon zu erwerben."

APRÈS ÊTRE DEVENU propriétaire de cet havre de paix de style bardeau à Southampton, ce globe-trotter fit l'acquisition des terres agricoles avoisinantes, reconfigura les parcelles, fit refaire la demeure principale de près de 640 mètres carrés puis plus tard fit construire une maison d'hôte de près de 510 mètres carrés à côté. Après avoir travaillé avec l'architecte basé dans le Connecticut, Richard Sawicki, maintenant décédé, sur les plans de la maison, il entreprit de meubler lui-même les intérieurs. « Pour moi, mon environnement c'est quelque chose de personnel et je veux m'y sentir à l'aise », nous dit le propriétaire. Et donc fort du confort comme élément moteur du décor, il remplit peu à peu les pièces des deux maisons avec du mobilier classique et des antiquités françaises et anglaises qu'il choisissait au cours de ses voyages. La palette reposante de tons neutres et le mobilier en majeure partie traditionnel sont pimentés d'œuvres d'art et d'éléments décoratifs hauts en couleurs dont une série de tableaux de Stefan Szczesny. « J'ai vu une exposition de son œuvre à Londres et j'ai appelé le peintre le jour suivant pour lui acheter toute sa série de tableaux. »

Vivid art and accents enliven the quiet palette with pops of color.

Die ruhige Tonpalette erhält durch die lebendige Kunst und die gesetzten Farbakzente Schwung.

Des œuvres d'art et des éléments décoratifs hauts en couleurs donnent vie à une palette tranquille en ajoutant des touches de couleur.

A sunny yellow fabric from Osborne & Little on the headboard and curtains adds warmth to a bedroom peppered with colonial-style furnishings and antiques.

Das mit sonnengelbem Stoff von Osborne & Little bezogene Kopfteil des Betts und die Vorhänge verleihen einem Schlafzimmer, das mit Möbeln und Antiquitäten im Kolonialstil ausgestattet ist, Wärme.

Un tissu jaune ensoleillé de Osborne & Little sur la tête de lit et les rideaux donne de la chaleur à une chambre parsemée de meubles et d'antiquités de style colonial.

Set at the corner of the property, the pool is anchored at one end by a pool house containing a kitchen and baths.

An einem Ende des Schwimmbeckens, das sich in einer Ecke des Grundstücks befindet, liegt ein Poolhaus mit einer Küche und Bädern.

En bord de la piscine à un coin de la propriété, se trouve une pergola renfermant une cuisine et des salles de bain.

Light House
Upper East Side

WHEN ARCHITECT Alexander Gorlin took on this 1957 townhouse's renovation, it was endowed with many positive attributes, including a glass facade and mid-century modern details. But the two-story home also had some drawbacks, such as a poorly conceived plan and limited light. Its owners also needed more space for their growing family. Gorlin set out to enlarge the home to 6,000 square feet by adding an extra floor and crowning it with a skylight. "We saved the existing travertine floors and elaborated on the better parts of the mid-century design, such as the updated staircase with its open risers, which let in extra light," says Gorlin, who also surrounded the staircase with glass block floors to allow even more natural illumination. Adding to the owners' existing collection of mid-century furniture, designer Emanuela Frattini Magnusson introduced an amalgam of new and vintage pieces to round out the modern mix.

ALS DER ARCHITEKT Alexander Gorlin den Auftrag übernahm, dieses Stadthaus aus dem Jahr 1957 zu renovieren, zeichnete es sich durch viele positive Merkmale aus, darunter eine Glasfassade und modernistische Details. Das zweistöckige Haus wies aber auch einige Nachteile auf, wie zum Beispiel einen schlecht durchdachten Raumplan und beschränkten Lichteinfall. Außerdem benötigten die Besitzer mehr Platz für ihre wachsende Familie. So begann Gorlin, die Wohnfläche des Hauses auf knapp 560 Quadratmeter zu vergrößern, indem er ein zusätzliches Stockwerk aufsetzte und es mit einem Dachfenster krönte. „Wir behielten die Travertinböden und verfeinerten die gelungeneren Teile des aus der Mitte des vorigen Jahrhunderts stammenden Entwurfs, wie zum Beispiel die erneuerte Treppe mit ihren offenen Setzstufen, durch die mehr Licht dringen kann", sagte Gorlin. Er fasste die an die Treppe angrenzenden Böden ebenfalls in Glasstein, damit noch mehr natürliches Licht einfallen kann. Die Innenarchitektin Emanuela Frattini Magnusson fügte der bereits bestehenden Sammlung von Möbeln neue und Vintage-Stücke hinzu, um die moderne Mischung abzurunden.

LORSQUE L'ARCHITECTE Alexander Gorlin s'attaqua à la rénovation de cette maison de ville datant de 1957, elle comptait de nombreux points positifs comme par exemple une façade de verre et des détails modernes des années 1950. Mais cette maison de deux étages avait aussi certains inconvénients comme une mauvaise conception dans les plans et un éclairage limité. Et les propriétaires avaient besoin de plus d'espace pour leur famille en pleine croissance. Gorlin entreprit d'agrandir la maison de près de 560 mètres carrés en ajoutant un étage supplémentaire surmonté d'une lucarne. « Nous avons conservé les sols de travertin et nous nous sommes consacrés à améliorer les meilleurs aspects de la conception des années 1950, comme la rénovation de l'escalier avec une finition ouverte qui laisse passer plus de lumière », nous dit Gorlin, qui a également entouré l'escalier d'un sol de blocs de verre pour permettre encore plus d'éclairage naturel. La décoratrice Emanuela Frattini Magnusson a ajouté un amalgame de pièces neuves et vintages à la collection de meubles des années 1950 des propriétaires qui complémentent parfaitement cet ensemble moderne.

Translucent cabinets in the kitchen contribute to the home's sense of airiness. White statuary marble lines the walls and floor of the master bath.

Durchsichtige Küchenschränke tragen zu dem luftigen Erscheinungsbild des Hauses bei. Die Wände und Böden im großen Badezimmer sind mit weißem Bildhauermarmor verkleidet.

Les armoires translucides dans la cuisine contribuent à donner un aspect aéré à la maison. Les murs et le sol de la salle de bains principale sont recouverts de marbre blanc statuaire.

A reconfigured fireplace and travertine floors set the mid-century modern tone in the living room. A new staircase with open risers lets in plenty of light.

Ein neu gestalteter Kamin und Travertinböden bestimmen den modernistischen Ton des Wohnzimmers. Eine neue Treppe mit offenen Setzstufen lässt viel Licht herein.

Une cheminée reconfigurée et des sols de travertin soulignent l'ambiance des années 1950 dans le séjour. Un nouvel escalier avec une finition ouverte laisse amplement passer la lumière.

Custom beech wood shelving and cabinets define the media room. The architect topped the newly added third floor with a skylight.

Maßgefertigte Buchenholzregale und -schränke kennzeichnen den Medienraum. Der Architekt krönte den neu hinzugefügten dritten Stock mit einem Dachfenster.

Des rayons et des armoires sur mesure en hêtre définissent la sale des médias. L'architecte a surmonté d'une lucarne le troisième étage qu'il venait d'ajouter.

Plaza Penthouse
Central Park South

IF TRUMAN CAPOTE were alive to see Dee and Tommy Hilfiger's 6,000-square-foot duplex penthouse in The Plaza Hotel, he'd probably be inspired to throw a party there. In fact, Capote occupies the dining room in the form of photographs taken at the legendary Black and White Ball he hosted in 1966. "Our inspiration was The Plaza and old-world New York," says Dee Hilfiger, who collaborated with designer Cindy Rinfret to define the interiors with a mix of antiques and architectural elements. Contemporary art collectors, they included works by Jean-Michel Basquiat and Andy Warhol. A highlight is the breakfast room, inspired by the children's book *Eloise at the Plaza*; the couple hired its illustrator, Hilary Knight, to create its fanciful murals. "It's one of my favorite rooms," says Hilfiger, noting that another cherished spot is the terrace off the master bedroom. "It has an insane view of Fifth Avenue and Central Park."

WÜRDE TRUMAN CAPOTE noch leben und das 550 Quadratmeter große Duplex-Penthouse von Dee und Tommy Hilfiger im Plaza Hotel sehen, wäre er wahrscheinlich versucht, dort eine Party zu geben. Capote ist tatsächlich im Esszimmer präsent, und zwar in Form von Fotografien vom legendären Schwarz-Weiß-Ball, dessen Gastgeber er 1966 war. „Das Plaza und die Welt des alten New York waren Inspirationen für uns", sagt Dee Hilfiger, die mit der Innenarchitektin Cindy Rinfret die Innenräume mit einer Mischung aus Antiquitäten und architektonischen Elementen ausstattete. In den Räumen der Sammler zeitgenössischer Kunst trifft man auch auf Werke von Jean-Michel Basquiat und Andy Warhol. Ein Glanzlicht ist das von dem Kinderbuch *Eloise im Plaza Hotel* inspirierte Frühstückszimmer: Das Paar beauftragte den Illustrator, Hilary Knight, fantasievolle Wandbilder zu schaffen. „Das ist einer meiner Lieblingsräume", so Hilfiger, und merkt an, dass die Terrasse vor dem großen Schlafzimmer ein weiterer, von ihm bevorzugter Ort ist. „Von dort aus hat man diesen wahnsinnigen Blick auf die Fifth Avenue und den Central Park."

SI TRUMAN CAPOTE était en vie et voyait le penthouse en duplex de près de 550 mètres carrés de Dee et Tommy Hilfiger dans le Plaza Hotel, il se sentirait probablement inspiré pour y organiser une fête. En fait, Capote occupe la salle à manger sous forme de photos prises lors du légendaire Bal noir et blanc qu'il avait organisé en 1966. « Notre source d'inspiration fut le Plaza et l'ancien New York », nous dit Dee Hilfiger, qui a collaboré avec la décoratrice Cindy Rinfret pour définir les intérieurs avec un mélange de pièces d'antiquité et d'éléments architecturaux. Collectionneurs d'art contemporain, ils ont ajouté des œuvres de Jean-Michel Basquiat et Andy Warhol. Un des points forts est la salle du petit déjeuner, inspirée du livre pour enfants *Eloïse au Plaza*. Le couple a engagé son illustratrice, Hilary Knight, pour créer ses merveilleux muraux. « C'est une de mes pièces préférées », nous dit Hilfiger, en soulignant qu'un autre de ses coins de prédilection est la terrasse de la chambre principale. « Elle offre une vue incroyable sur la Cinquième Avenue et Central Park. »

Art by Keith Haring, Jean-Michel Basquiat, and Andy Warhol brings vibrant notes of contrast to rooms defined by antique furnishings and classic elements.

Kunstwerke von Keith Haring, Jean-Michel Basquiat und Andy Warhol erzeugen dynamische Gegensätze in den Räumen, die sich durch antike Möbel und klassische Elemente auszeichnen.

Des œuvres d'art de Keith Haring, Jean-Michel Basquiat et Andy Warhol apportent des touches intenses de contraste aux chambres agrémentées de meubles anciens et d'éléments classiques.

The Hilfigers' son's room features a nautical theme.

Das Zimmer des Sohns der Hilfigers durchzieht ein maritimes Thema.

La chambre du fils des Hilfiger présente un thème nautique.

Quilted black leather warms the powder room's walls and black-and-white photographs add flavor to a guest room.

Gestepptes schwarzes Leder verleiht den Wänden der Damentoilette Wärme, während Schwarz-Weiß-Fotografien zur Atmosphäre eines Gästezimmers beitragen.

Du cuir matelassé noir donne un air douillet aux murs de la salle d'eau et des photos en noir et blanc apporte un cachet à la chambre d'ami.

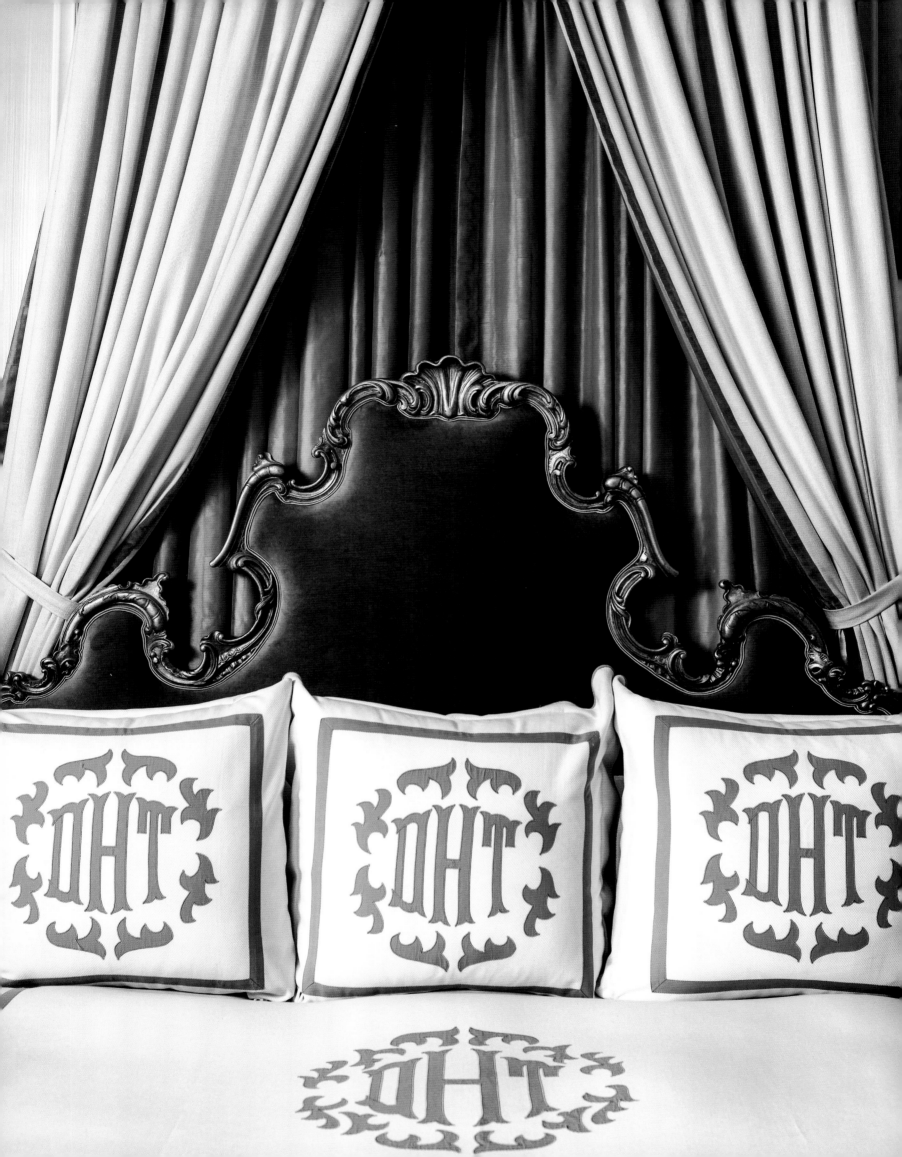

An antique headboard was reupholstered in gray velvet in the master bedroom. The fireplace and chandelier were found in an antiques shop in New York.

Ein antikes Kopfende wurde im großen Schlafzimmer mit grauem Samt neu gepolstert. Den Kamin und den Leuchter fand man in einem Antiquitätengeschäft in New York.

La tête de lit ancienne dans la chambre principale a été retapissée en velours gris. La cheminée et le lustre font partie des trouvailles chez les antiquaires de New York.

An art deco vanity occupies a niche off the master bedroom and the closet features black lacquer shelves and doors.

Ein Art-déco-Waschtisch füllt eine Nische neben dem großen Schlafzimmer aus, während der begehbare Kleider-schrank schwarze Lackregale und -türen aufweist.

Une coiffeuse art déco occupe un renforcement en sortant de la salle de bains et le placard présente des rayons et des portes en noir laqué.

The breakfast room—situated beneath a dome at the top of The Plaza—was fancifully adorned with murals by Hilary Knight, the illustrator of the children's book Eloise at the Plaza.

Das Frühstückszimmer, das sich in einem kuppelför- migen Aufbau oben auf dem Plaza befindet, wurde mit Wandgemälden von Hilary Knight, dem Illustrator des Kinderbuchs Eloise im Plaza Hotel, *fantasievoll ausgeschmückt.*

La salle du petit déjeuner située en dessous du dôme au sommet du Plaza est magnifiquement décorée avec des muraux de Hilary Knight, l'illustratrice du livre pour enfants, Eloïse au Plaza.

The kitchen counters are made of Carrara marble. The dining room ceiling was finished in gold leaf and inlaid chairs from India surround the Maison Jansen table.

Die Küchenoberflächen bestehen aus Carrara-Marmor. Die Decke im Esszimmer wurde mit Blattgold überzogen, während Stühle mit Intarsien aus Indien sich um den Tisch von Maison Jansen gruppieren.

Les plans de travail de la cuisine sont en marbre de Carrare. Le plafond de la salle à manger a des finitions de doré à la feuille et des chaises incrustées venant de l'Inde autour de la table de la Maison Jansen.

High Line Living
Chelsea

WHEN DESIGNER Sandra Chamberlin entered the 2,500-square-foot apartment in the Neil Denari–designed HL23, a condominium building next to Manhattan's High Line Park, her first thought was to leave it exactly as it was. "I'm a minimalist and felt this is how it should remain—empty." Leaving it as such wasn't an option, since the owners desired a family-friendly home. Among the major strokes she undertook to transform the space were commandeering a third bedroom to create a new kitchen and crafting a vertical garden on one wall. The yellow and gray kitchen/family area was made kid-friendly by adding a banquette that wraps around two sides. Its breakfast bar has become the central gathering spot when the family entertains. A final bonus was the clients' relationship with the architect and artist Maya Lin, whose favorite lighting designers conceived custom fixtures that bring the happy home an extra shot of sparkle.

ALS DIE INNENARCHITEKTIN Sandra Chamberlin das 230 Quadratmeter große Apartment im von Neil Denari entworfenen HL23 betrat, ein juwelenartiges Gebäude mit Eigentumswohnungen neben dem High Line Park in Manhattan, war ihr erster Gedanke, es genau so zu belassen, wie es war. „Ich bin Minimalistin und fand, es sollte so bleiben, wie es ist – leer." Dies stand allerdings nicht zur Debatte, da sich die Besitzer ein familienfreundliches Zuhause wünschten. Wesentliche Veränderungen waren, das dritte Schlafzimmer in eine neue Küche zu verwandeln und eine der Wände mit einem vertikalen Garten zu versehen. Der gelbe und grüne Küchen- und Familienbereich wurde mit einer an beiden Seiten abgerundeten Sitzbank kinderfreundlich umgestaltet. Die Frühstückstheke ist zum zentralen Ort geworden, an dem sich alle versammeln, wenn die Familie Gäste bewirtet. Ein Pluspunkt war zuletzt auch die Bekanntschaft des Bauherrn mit der Architektin und Künstlerin Maya Lin, deren Lieblingslichtdesigner maßgeschneiderte Beleuchtungskörper konzipierte, die dem glücklichen Zuhause zusätzlich Glanz verleihen.

LORSQUE LA DÉCORATRICE Sandra Chamberlin entra dans cet appartement de près de 230 mètres carrés au douzième étage du HL23, un appartement en copropriété à côté du High Line Park à Manhattan, conçu par Neil Denari, elle pensa d'abord à le laisser absolument tel quel. « Je suis une minimaliste et je pensais que c'était ainsi qu'il devait rester, vide. » Mais le laisser tel quel était hors de question du fait que les propriétaires souhaitaient une demeure familiale accueillante. Parmi les principales étapes qu'elle entreprit pour transformer l'espace fut de réquisitionner la troisième chambre pour créer une nouvelle cuisine et d'ajouter un jardin vertical sur un mur. La cuisine/séjour familial en jaune et gris est accueillante pour les enfants en raison d'une banquette qui va autour de deux côtés. Le bar du petit déjeuner est devenu l'espace central de réunion pour recevoir. Et en prime il y eut la relation des clients avec l'architecte et artiste, Maya Lin, qui s'arrangea pour que ses spécialistes préférés de l'éclairage conçoivent des jeux de lumière qui apportent une ultime touche scintillante à cette demeure joyeuse.

The "plant wall" by Laurent Corradi is a living, breathing, mechanized, system made up of plumbing pipes, felt pockets, timers, liquid food, mixers, and about 350 plants. A pair of chairs covered in colorful suede petals extends the plant wall's color and texture into the living space.

Die „Pflanzenwand" von Laurent Corradi ist ein lebendiges, atmendes, automatisiertes System mit Rohren, Filztaschen, Zeitschaltuhren, Flüssignahrung, Mischern und ungefähr 350 Pflanzen. Zwei Sessel, die mit bunten Blütenblättern aus Wildleder bezogen sind, führen die farbige Pflanzenwand in den Wohnraum fort.

Le « mur de plantes » de Laurent Corradi est un système vivant et mécanisé qui respire, fait avec des tuyaux, des poches de feutre, une minuterie, des aliments liquides, des mélangeurs et près de 350 plantes. Une paire de chaises couvertes de pétales en daim chatoyant prolongent la couleur et la texture du mur de plantes dans le séjour.

Livable Luxe
Upper East Side

AFTER DESIGNING OTHER homes for the owners of this Fifth Avenue co-op, designer John Willey had secured his clients' "full trust," so he was free to take a fresh direction. Though the 3,200-square-foot, apartment brims with lovely pre-war details, its interiors were "stodgy," says the designer, "so I gave it a facelift for a more youthful character." His first step was to solve some of the space issues. "Once I got the bones in beautiful shape, then I could complement the dynamic rooms to bring it to life," Willey explains. Here, he restricted the fabrics to solids in five colors—black, gray, ivory, pale blue, and a dose of cranberry—and bleached the original oak floors to a Scandinavian gray, giving the residence a dreamy lightness. A thoughtful mix of custom-designed furniture and vintage pieces features playful takes on some English traditions, "like a tête-à-tête sofa or swag drapery with tiebacks" to infuse the rooms with "big-city glamour."

NACHDEM DER INNENARCHITEKT John Willey bereits andere Häuser der Besitzer dieser Wohnung auf der Fifth Avenue gestaltet und so deren „vollstes Vertrauen" erworben hatte, ließen ihm seine Auftraggeber freie Hand, um eine neue Richtung einzuschlagen. Auch wenn das knapp 300 Quadratmeter große Apartment über zahlreiche liebenswerte Details aus der Vorkriegszeit verfügte, waren die Innenräume „langweilig", so der Innenarchitekt, „weshalb ich ihnen ein neues Gesicht mit einem jugendlicheren Charakter verlieh". Zuerst machte er sich an die Lösung einiger Raumprobleme. „Nachdem ich die Hülle wunderbar in Form gebracht hatte, konnte ich beginnen, den dynamischen Räumen Leben einzuhauchen", erklärt Willey. Er beschränkte sich bei den Stoffen und der Einrichtung auf fünf Farben – Schwarz, Grau, Elfenbein, Hellblau und hier und da eine Spur von Preiselbeere – und bleichte die ursprünglichen Eichenholzböden in skandinavisches Grau, sodass die Wohnung eine verträumte Leichtigkeit erhielt. Eine sorgfältige Mischung aus maßgefertigten Möbeln und Vintage-Stücken weist eine verspielte Herangehensweise an einige englische Traditionen auf, „wie zum Beispiel ein Tête-à-Tête-Sofa oder seitlich geraffte Vorhänge", um den Räumen „Großstadtglamour" zu verleihen.

APRÈS AVOIR CONÇU d'autres demeures pour les propriétaires de cet appartement coopératif sur la Cinquième Avenue, le décorateur John Willey s'était gagné la « pleine confiance » de ses clients et il avait donc toute liberté pour décider d'une nouvelle direction. Bien que l'appartement de près de 300 mètres carrés débordait de charmants détails d'avant-guerre, ses intérieurs étaient « patauds », nous dit le décorateur, « et c'est ainsi que je lui ai fait un lifting pour lui donner un air de jeunesse ». La première étape fut de résoudre certains problèmes de place. « Après avoir obtenu une solide ossature, je pouvais ajouter des chambres dynamiques pour lui donner vie », nous explique Willey. Là il s'est limité à cinq couleurs unies pour les tissus : noir, gris, ivoire, bleu clair et une dose de groseille, puis il a blanchi les planchers d'origine en chêne pour obtenir un gris scandinave et donner une légèreté de rêve à la résidence. Un mélange bien pensé de meubles faits sur mesure et de pièces vintage sont un clin d'œil à la tradition anglaise « comme un canapé tête-à-tête ou des tentures retenues par des cordons » pour apporter le « glamour de la grande ville aux chambres ».

The fabrics in the living room include mohair, linen, chenille, leather, and velvet.

Die Stoffe im Wohnzimmer umfassen Mohair, Leinen, Chenille, Leder und Samt.

Les tissus du séjour comprennent le mohair, le lin, la chenille, le cuir et le velours.

Playfulness and substance merge throughout, even in the kitchen—with its limestone floors, plaster details, and wallpapered ceiling.

Verspieltheit und Sachlichkeit verschmelzen in sämtlichen Räumen miteinander, selbst in der Küche mit ihren Kalksteinböden, den Stuckdetails und der tapezierten Decke.

Esprit ludique et profondeur se mélangent sans cesse, même dans la cuisine avec un sol en calcaire, des détails de stuc et un plafond recouvert de papier peint.

Integrated millwork in the bedroom and the bath's vanity were discretely incorporated for storage.

Der Einbauschrank im Schlafzimmer und der Waschtisch im Bad wurden dezent in die Räume eingefügt.

Des pièces de menuiserie intégrées dans la chambre et l'armoire de la salle de bains furent ajoutées discrètement pour les rangements.

Contemporary art and furnishings are mixed with vintage pieces, including a circa 1955 chrome and Lucite ceiling pendant by Gaetano Sciolari in the media room.

Zeitgenössische Kunst und Möbel werden mit Vintage-Stücken gemischt, darunter eine im Medienraum hängende Deckenlampe aus Chrom und Plexiglas von Gaetano Sciolari, die ungefähr aus dem Jahr 1955 stammt.

Des œuvres d'art et un mobilier contemporains sont mélangés à des pièces vintage comme une lampe suspendue au plafond en chrome et lucite datant de 1955 signée Gaetano Sciolari dans la salle des médias.

Summer Escape

East Hampton

AFTER A LONG work week, the owner of this 9,000-square-foot house in East Hampton takes refuge in its cozy rooms. With a twist on the classic beach vernacular, Dominic Gasparoly and Khalid Watson of GWdesign sought to radiate a spirit of ease throughout. "This is not a typical Hamptons house," explains Gasparoly. "Contemporary elements play off 'revised' classic pieces." From the double-height foyer to a driftwood sculpture, every space was conceived around comfort. Custom furnishings and accents, such as the reclaimed-wood dining table or the bentwood chandelier, link the interiors with their beach-y context. Contrasting with the upper levels' sunny effervescence, the basement offers a "chic take on the man cave." Equipped with a gym, sauna, and steam shower, along with a red-curtained lounge and fifteen-seat theater, this, says Gasparoly, "is undoubtedly the most fun portion of the house."

NACH EINER LANGEN Woche zieht sich der Besitzer dieses 850 Quadratmeter großen Hauses in East Hampton in seine gemütlichen Räume zurück. Dominic Gasparoly und Khalid Watson von GWdesign waren bestrebt, der klassischen Bauweise eines Strandhauses das gewisse Etwas zu verleihen. „Das ist kein typisches Haus in den Hamptons", erklärt Gasparoly. „Moderne Elemente stehen ‚überarbeiteten' klassischen Stücken gegenüber." Von der zweigeschossigen Eingangshalle bis hin zu einer Skulptur aus Treibholz wurden sämtliche Räume so konzipiert, dass sie Behaglichkeit verströmen. Die nach den Wünschen des Kunden angefertigte Einrichtung und die gesetzten Akzente – wie zum Beispiel der Esstisch aus aufgearbeitetem Holz oder der Leuchter aus Bugholz – verweisen auf das maritime Umfeld. Im Gegensatz zum sonnigen Erscheinungsbild der oberen Stockwerke zeigt das Untergeschoss eine „stilvolle Herangehensweise an die Höhle des Mannes". Ausgestattet mit einem Fitnessstudio, einer Sauna, einer Dampfdusche sowie einer mit roten Vorhängen versehenen Lounge und einem fünfzehn Plätze umfassenden Kino ist dieser Teil des Hauses, so Gasparoly, „zweifellos derjenige, der das größte Vergnügen bietet".

APRÈS UNE LONGUE semaine de travail, le propriétaire de cette maison de près de 850 mètres carrés à East Hampton peut se réfugier dans ses chambres douillettes. Pour donner une touche originale à la classique maison de plage, Dominic Gasparoly et Khalid Watson de GWdesign ont cherché à transmettre une atmosphère décontractée partout. « Ce n'est pas la maison typique des Hamptons », nous explique Gasparoly. « Des éléments contemporains soulignent des pièces classiques 'revues'. » De l'entrée aérée à double hauteur à une sculpture en bois de grève, chaque espace a été conçu en tenant compte du confort. Le mobilier et les objets décoratifs sur mesure comme la grande table en bois de récupération ou le lustre en bois courbé, relient les espaces intérieurs au contexte de la plage. En contraste avec l'effervescence ensoleillée des niveaux supérieurs, l'étage du dessous propose « une touche chic pour la caverne de l'homme ». Equipée d'une salle de gym, d'un sauna et d'une douche à vapeur, ainsi que d'un salon avec des rideaux rouges et un théâtre à quinze places, c'est, nous dit Gasparoly, « sans doute la partie la plus joyeuse de la maison ».

The custom circular chandelier in the foyer conceals both lights and speakers. Encasing the family room's fireplace within a mantel and then facing it with a black glass panel allows the TV to disappear when it's not turned on.

In dem nach den Wünschen des Kunden gefertigten runden Leuchter in der Eingangshalle verstecken sich sowohl Lampen als auch Lautsprecherboxen. Eine besondere Ummantelung des Kamins lässt den Fernseher verschwinden, wenn er nicht eingeschaltet ist.

Le lustre circulaire sur mesure dans l'entrée cache les lumières et les speakers. Un système encastré spécial dans la cheminée fait disparaitre la télévision lorsqu'elle est éteinte.

A refined, sun-bleached palette and understated nautical references infuse the kitchen and dining room with a sophisticated yet relaxed beach house flavor.

Eine feine, sonnengebleichte Farbpalette und dezente nautische Bezüge erfüllen die Küche und das Esszimmer mit einer raffinierten, aber dennoch entspannten Strandhausatmosphäre.

Une palette raffinée de tons décolorés par le soleil et des références nautiques discrètes diffusent une touche de maison de plage à la fois raffinée et décontractée dans la cuisine et la salle à manger.

The fireplace in the living room is faced with crema marfil *and Corinthian Beige marble in a brick pattern of varying heights and finishes. A vintage sailboat sits atop a custom console made of riff-sawn Italian and American walnut.*

Der Kamin im Wohnzimmer ist mit dem Marmor Crema Marfil und Corinthian Beige verkleidet, und weist ein Ziegelsteinmuster mit unterschiedlichen Höhen und Schattierungen auf. Ein Vintage-Segelboot befindet sich auf einer maßgefertigten Konsole aus italienischem und amerikanischem Walnussholz.

La cheminée dans le salon est recouverte de marbre crema marfil *et de marbre de Corinthe beige avec un motif de briques de différentes hauteurs et finitions. Un bateau à voiles vintage est posé sur une console en bois de noyer italien et américain faite sur mesure.*

Beach-inspired accents, including an authentic wooden propeller and a piece of driftwood on a metal base, add subtle coastal flavor to the master bedroom and a guest bedroom.

Von der Strandumgebung inspirierte Akzente, darunter ein echter Holzpropeller und ein Stück Treibholz auf einem Metallständer, verleihen dem großen Schlafzimmer und einem Gästeschlafzimmer eine dezente Küstennote.

Les touches inspirées par la plage dont une hélice en bois authentique et un morceau de bois de grève sur une base de métal ajoutent un petit goût subtil d'ambiance côtière à la chambre principale et une chambre d'ami.

The designers converted the basement into a chic "man cave," defining it with a full-scale gym, a sultry pool hall, and a fifteen-seat home theater.

Die Innenarchitekten verwandelten das Untergeschoss in eine stilvolle „Höhle des Mannes" und grenzten es mit einem vollständig ausgestatteten Fitnessstudio, einem sinnlichen Billardzimmer und einem fünfzehn Plätze umfassenden Heimkino vom Rest des Hauses ab.

Les décorateurs ont transformé le sous-sol en une « caverne de l'homme » chic et l'ont personnalisée avec une salle de remise en forme complète, une salle de billard irrésistible et un théâtre maison à quinze places.

A Touch of Glamour
Upper East Side

"MOST CALL THIS apartment 'swanky,'" says designer Brenda Exline of the duplex penthouse she designed for herself and her husband. Inspired by glamorous French style, Exline crafted a 4,300-square-foot masterpiece brimming with exquisite elements, exceptional antiques, and contemporary accents. "We bought two apartments after we got married and wanted to make them our 'love nest in the sky,'" Exline reveals. This explains the palette of robin's egg blue, brown, taupe, and beige. Before Exline began feathering this elegant nest, she collaborated with architect Guillermo M. Gomez and Jeff Lincoln Interiors to merge the penthouses, gut them almost to thin "air," and rebuild them from scratch. Now known as Hardt House, the designer says she "Americanized" the original European elements by "topping them off with creative whimsy for a bit of fun." The result: an Upper East Side trophy.

„DIE MENSCHEN BEZEICHNEN dieses Apartment als ‚protzig'", sagt die Designerin Brenda Exline von dem Duplex-Penthouse, das sie für sich und ihren Mann gestaltete. Inspiriert vom französischen Stil, schuf Exline ein 400 Quadratmeter großes Meisterwerk voller außergewöhnlicher Antiquitäten und mit zeitgenössischen Wohnakzenten. „Gleich nach unserer Hochzeit kauften wir zwei Penthouse-Wohnungen, um sie in ein ‚himmlisches Liebesnest' für uns zu verwandeln", offenbart Exline. Das erklärt die in den Innenräumen vorherrschende Farbpalette von Eierschalenblau, Braun, Taupe und Beige. Zuvor arbeitete sie mit dem Architekturbüro Guillermo M. Gomez and Jeff Lincoln Interiors zusammen, das die beiden Wohnungen zusammenführte. Sie ließ diese soweit entkernen, dass sie sich quasi in „Luft" auflösten, und baute sie aus diesem Nichts wieder auf. Die Innenarchitektin sagt von dem mittlerweile als Hardt House bekannten Gebäude, dass sie die ursprünglich europäischen Elemente „amerikanisierte", indem sie sie „aus Spaß mit einem rätselhaften, kreativen Spleen versah". Das Ergebnis: ein Schmuckstück an der Upper East Side.

« LA PLUPART DES gens disent que cet appartement est 'ultrachic' », nous annonce Brenda Exline, la décoratrice de ce penthouse en duplex qu'elle a conçu pour elle-même et son mari. Inspirée par le style glamour français, Exline a produit une pièce maîtresse d'environ 400 mètres carrés qui regorge de détails architecturaux exquis, des pièces d'antiquité et des touches contemporaines exceptionnelles. « Nous avons acheté deux appartements après notre mariage et nous voulions en faire notre 'nid d'amour dans le ciel' », nous dit Exline, ce qui explique la palette avec un bleu-vert comme des œufs de merle et les bruns et les beiges. Avant de commencer à remplumer ce nid élégant, Exline a collaboré avec l'architecte Guillermo M. Gomez et Jeff Lincoln Interiors pour fusionner les penthouses qui furent éventrés et réduits à presque rien, puis reconstruits. Connu sous le nom de Hardt House, la décoratrice nous dit qu'elle a « américanisé » les éléments européens en « ajoutant des éléments créatifs et fééeriques pour s'amuser un peu ». Le résultat : un trophée dans l'Upper East Side.

Paul Mathieu's stunning hand-blown glass chandelier illuminates the custom Macassar and nickel table in the dining room. Hervé Van der Straeten's handmade bronze bull's-eye mirror reflects light and adds esoteric sparkle.

Paul Mathieus atemberaubender mundgeblasener Kronleuchter aus Glas beleuchtet den maßgefertigten Tisch aus Makassar-Ebenholz und Nickel im Esszimmer. Hervé Van der Straetens handgefertigter runder Spiegel aus Bronze reflektiert das Licht und verleiht dem Raum zusätzlich eine esoterische Note.

Un lustre extraordinaire en verre soufflé bouche de Paul Mathieu illumine la table sur mesure en Macassar et nickel dans la salle à manger. Le miroir artisanal œil de bœuf en bronze d'Hervé Van der Straeten reflète la lumière et ajoute un éclat ésotérique.

Upon entering the penthouse, the first thing one sees is the massive custom mahogany-and-bronze 1920s-inspired spiral staircase in front of a two-story, 20-foot-high window.

Bevor man das Penthouse betritt, erblickt man zuerst die von den 1920er-Jahren inspirierte, maßgefertigte Wendeltreppe aus Mahagoni und Bronze vor einem 6 Meter hohen zweigeschossigen Fenster.

En entrant dans le penthouse, la première chose que vous voyez c'est l'immense escalier en spirale, acajou et bronze, inspiré des années 1920 face à une fenêtre sur deux étages de plus de 6 mètres de haut.

Fur rugs and throws and custom canopied beds radiate warmth and glamour in the bedrooms.

Hochflorteppiche, Überwürfe und maßgefertigte Himmelbetten verströmen Wärme und Glanz in den Schlafzimmern.

Des tapis et des plaids de fourrure et des lits à baldaquins faits sur mesure apportent de la chaleur et du glamour dans les chambres.

French Connection

Upper East Side

AFTER THEY MARRIED, hairdresser Frédéric Fekkai and his wife, Shirin von Wulffen, purchased their first home together—a duplex overlooking Central Park. Given their international backgrounds—von Wulffen is German, raised in Iran and Virginia, and Fekkai is French of Vietnamese and Egyptian descent—the couple sought to fuse their tastes by referencing elements of their past. To help shape their rooms, they turned to Fekkai's longtime friend, French-born interior designer Robert Couturier. The couple and Couturier share a sense of adventure and an eye for beauty, so they took trips to France together, yielding much of the art and furniture that fills their home. Couturier kept the ambiance fun by adding eighteenth-century antiques and pop art amid a palette of rich jewel tones. Anchoring the mélange are a few Persian rugs that weave another intonation of the couple's history into their happy present.

NACH IHRER HEIRAT kauften der Starfriseur Frédéric Fekkai und seine Frau Shirin von Wulffen ihr erstes gemeinsames Zuhause – eine Maisonette mit Blick auf den Central Park. Aufgrund ihrer internationalen Herkunft – von Wulffen ist eine im Iran und in Virginia aufgewachsene Deutsche, während Fekkai aus Frankreich stammt und vietnamesisch-ägyptische Vorfahren hat – nahm das Paar auf Elemente ihrer Herkunft Bezug. Für die Ausgestaltung der Räume wandten sie sich an Fekkais langjährigen Freund, den in Frankreich geborenen Innenarchitekten Robert Couturier. Das Paar und Couturier teilen den Sinn für das Abenteuer und den Blick für das Schöne und unternahmen mehrfach Reisen nach Frankreich, von denen sie viele Kunstwerke und Möbelstücke mitbrachten. Couturier behielt die lebhafte Atmosphäre mit ihren klaren Tönen bei und platzierte darin Antiquitäten aus dem achtzehnten Jahrhundert und Pop-Art. Die Mischung wird durch einige Perserteppiche unterstrichen, die die Vergangenheit des Paares mit ihrem jetzigen, glücklichen Dasein verknüpfen.

APRÈS LEUR MARIAGE, le coiffeur Frédéric Fekkai et sa femme, Shirin von Wulffen, firent l'acquisition de leur première demeure, un duplex donnant sur Central Park. En raison de leurs origines internationales (von Wulffen est allemande et a grandi en Iran et en Virginie et Fekkai est français d'origine vietnamienne et égyptienne) le couple a souhaité fusionner leurs goûts éclectiques en faisant appel à des éléments de leur passé. Ils se tournèrent vers un ami de longue date de Fekkai, le décorateur d'intérieur né en France, Robert Couturier, pour qu'il les aide à créer le décor des chambres. Le couple et Couturier partageaient un sens de l'aventure sans perdre de vue l'esthétique et donc ils ont fait plusieurs voyages en France où ils ont déniché la plus grande partie des œuvres d'art et du mobilier qui se trouve dans leur appartement. Couturier a conservé une ambiance joyeuse en ajoutant des pièces d'antiquité du XVIIIe siècle et du pop art dans une palette de tons chaleureux. L'ensemble est agrémenté de quelques tapis persans qui transmettent un aspect de l'histoire du couple et racontent leur bonheur présent.

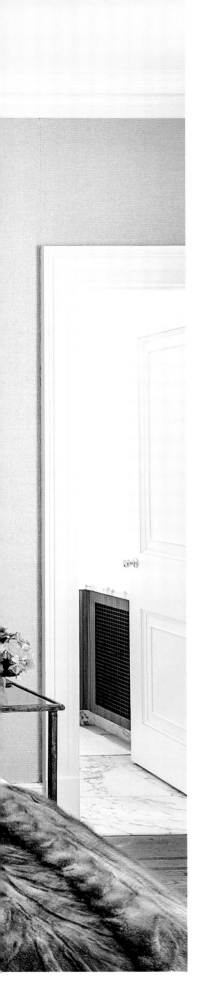

As in many Parisian apartments, antiques are mixed with vintage and contemporary furnishings, including eighteenth-century chairs, 1950s cloisonné lamps, and a set of cocktail tables by Mattia Bonetti in the living room.

So wie in vielen Pariser Wohnungen werden auch in diesem Wohnzimmer Antiquitäten mit modernem Mobiliar und Vintage-Möbeln kombiniert. Hier sind es Stühle aus dem achtzehnten Jahrhundert mit Cloisonné-Lampen aus den 1950er-Jahren und einem Satz Couchtische von Mattia Bonetti.

Tout comme dans de nombreux appartements parisiens, les antiquités côtoient des meubles vintages et contemporains comme des sièges du dix-huitième, des lampes 1950 en cloisonné et un ensemble de tables de cocktail signé Mattia Bonetti dans le séjour.

A modern Hervé Van der Straeten steel console and a Tommi Parzinger mirror pep up the traditional detailing in the hallway, while the Maurice Calka "boomerang" desk and vintage chair add zing to the library/home office.

Eine moderne Konsole aus Stahl von Hervé Van der Straeten und ein Spiegel von Tommi Parzinger lockern den traditionell gestalteten Eingang auf, während der „Boomerang"-Schreibtisch von Maurice Calka und der Vintage-Stuhl dem kombinierten Raum aus Bibliothek und Arbeitszimmer Pfiff verleihen.

Une console moderne en acier d'Hervé Van der Straeten et un miroir de Tommi Parzinger ajoutent un grain de sel au décor traditionnel du couloir et le bureau « boomerang » et le fauteuil vintage de Maurice Calka donnent du piquant à la bibliothèque/bureau.

An Hervé Van der Straeten chandelier hangs above a 1988 Italian table surrounded by Louis XVI-style chairs in the dining room. The kitchen is understated and cozy.

Ein Leuchter von Hervé Van der Straeten hängt im Esszimmer über einem italienischen Tisch von 1988, um den sich Stühle im Stil Louis XVI gruppieren. Die Küche ist dezent und gemütlich.

Un lustre d'Hervé Van der Straeten pend au-dessus d'une table italienne de 1988 entourée par des chaises Louis XVI dans la salle à manger. La cuisine est sobre et accueillante.

East Meets East
Upper East Side

UPON MOVING BACK to New York after living in Hong Kong, the couple living in this Park Avenue duplex wanted to bring intonations of the Asian ambience they'd grown accustomed to into their Manhattan home. To merge aspects of the Far East with the classic prewar details in their 4,200-square-foot Upper East Side co-op, they enlisted interior designer Campion Platt, who opened the traditional plan to create a series of layers that evoke an Asian-inspired, easy-living home. "Our goal was to create a warm, soothing environment of high visual contrast between light and dark, the rich wood of the Chinese furniture mingled with the soft neutral tones of the fabrics," says the designer. To set the elegant tone, the designer employed a rich English brown oak for cabinets in the main areas. In contrast, he played up the Asian spirit in the private spaces with different materials, such as anigre wood, in the master suite. "The exotic soft-grained wood really helped nail the modern Asian feel."

ALS DAS PAAR, das in dieser Maisonette auf der Park Avenue wohnt, von Hongkong zurück nach New York zog, wollte es seinem Wohnsitz in Manhattan eine asiatische Note verleihen, da es sich während seines Aufenthalts im Fernen Osten an das dortige Ambiente gewöhnt hatte. Um die fernöstlichen Bezüge mit den klassischen Details ihrer aus der Vorkriegszeit stammenden, 400 Quadratmeter großen Wohnung zu vereinen, beauftragten sie den Innenarchitekten Campion Platt, der die herkömmliche Raumaufteilung aufbrach, um eine Abfolge von Räumen zu schaffen, die ihr Heim asiatisch anmuten und in dem es sich einfach und bequem leben lässt. „Unser Ziel war es, eine warme, beruhigende Umgebung mit großen, sichtbaren Gegensätzen von hell und dunkel zu schaffen, in der sich die prächtigen chinesischen Möbel mit den weichen neutralen Tönen der Stoffe mischen", erklärt der Innenarchitekt. Um die elegante Note zu erreichen, verwendete er kräftige, braune englische Eiche in den Hauptwohnbereichen, während er die asiatische Stimmung in den privaten Räumen mit verschiedenen Materialien wie zum Beispiel Anigre-Holz in der Mastersuite betonte. „Das exotische, zart gemaserte Holz half, diese moderne asiatische Atmosphäre zu schaffen."

APRÈS AVOIR VÉCU à Hong Kong ce couple est revenu à New York dans leur duplex de Park Avenue et ils ont voulu transplanter dans leur demeure à Manhattan quelques notes de l'ambiance asiatique à laquelle ils s'étaient habitués. Ils firent appel au décorateur Campion Platt pour une fusion de l'Extrême-Orient avec les détails classiques d'avant-guerre de leur appartement en copropriété de près de 400 mètres carrés dans l'Upper East Side. Campion Platt ouvrit l'aménagement traditionnel pour créer une série de superpositions qui évoquent une maison facile à vivre inspirée par l'Asie. « Notre objectif était de créer un environnement chaleureux et apaisant avec de forts contrastes visuels entre le clair et le foncé, les bois luxuriants des meubles chinois mariés aux tons neutres et doux des tissus », nous dit le décorateur. Pour donner un air d'élégance, il utilisa du chêne foncé intense pour les armoires dans les espaces principaux. Par contraste, les espaces privés évoquent un esprit venu d'Asie avec des matières différentes comme le bois d'anigre dans la chambre principale. « Ce bois exotique à grain fin apporte réellement cet esprit asiatique moderne. »

English brown oak cabinets in the foyer and other traditional elements in the kitchen and dining room harmonize with Asian accents.

Schränke aus brauner englischer Eiche in der Diele und andere traditionelle Elemente in der Küche und im Esszimmer ergeben ein harmonisches Bild mit den asiatischen Akzenten, die gesetzt wurden.

Les armoires anglaises en chêne foncé dans l'entrée et d'autres éléments traditionnels dans la cuisine et la salle à manger s'harmonisent avec des touches d'Asie.

Anigre millwork and a pair of antique Chinese chairs set a serene Asian tone in the master suite.

Anigre-Holzbauteile und zwei antike chinesische Stühle verleihen der Mastersuite eine ruhige asiatische Note.

La boiserie d'anigre et une paire de fauteuils chinois antiques apportent un air de sérénité à la chambre principale.

Style, Underground
TriBeCa

FASHION DESIGNER Lela Rose's family loves to entertain in this 5,800-square-foot "inverse triplex" in TriBeCa. So when they enlisted WORKac to transform the levels of the historic building, they asked them to create a variety of spaces for their multifaceted lifestyle. They demolished the floors and reconstructed them to allow for three full-height levels. At street level, a loft-like living area with white resin floors and 16-foot-high ceilings adjoins a bamboo-lined box with motorized tables that rise for Japanese-style dining. The kitchen/dining area houses a formal table and a media room provides a comfy nook with a "kids-only" sleeping loft. To bring light into the lower sleeping levels, they installed an industrial-style skylight. Even the dogs, who have their own doghouse/elevator, were considered in this nuanced home.

DIE FAMILIE DER Modedesignerin Lela Rose liebt es, Gäste in ihrem 550 Quadratmeter großen Triplex-Apartment in TriBeCa zu empfangen. Sie baten das Architekturbüro WORKac, auf den verschiedenen Etagen unterschiedliche Räume für ihren facettenreichen Lebensstil zu schaffen. Die Untergeschosse wurden entkernt und wieder so aufgebaut, dass das Apartment drei hohe Etagen bekam. Das Stockwerk auf Straßenniveau beherbergt einen loftähnlichen Wohnbereich, der mit Harzböden und knapp 5 Meter hohen Wänden versehen ist. Daran schließt sich ein mit Bambusholz verkleideter offener Kubus mit versenkbaren Tischen an, die für Essen im japanischen Stil herausgefahren werden können. Ein klassischer Esstisch befindet sich noch im Küchen- und Essbereich, und im Medienraum gibt es eine gemütliche Ecke mit einem Schlafboden „nur für Kinder". Um die unteren Schlafzimmer mit Licht zu versorgen, wurde ein großflächiges Oberlicht im Industriestil eingebaut. Selbst die Hunde wurden in die Überlegungen für dieses ausgeklügelte Heim miteinbezogen: Sie besitzen eine Hundehütte mit eigenem Aufzug.

LA FAMILLE DE la créatrice de mode, Lela Rose, aime recevoir dans ce « triplex inversé » de près de 550 mètres carrés à TriBeCa. Et donc lorsqu'ils firent appel à WORKac pour transformer les niveaux de cet immeuble historique, ils leur demandèrent de créer toute une série d'espaces pour leur style de vie à facettes multiples. Ils démolirent et reconstruisirent le plancher pour obtenir trois niveaux à pleine hauteur. Au niveau de la rue, un séjour de type loft avec des planchers en résine blanche et des plafonds de plus de 5 mètres est adjacent à un box revêtu de bambou avec des tables motorisées qui surgissent pour dîner à la japonaise. L'espace cuisine/salle à manger abrite une grande table classique et une salle des médias qui offre un coin douillet avec un loft pour dormir « réservé aux enfants ». Ils installèrent une lucarne de style industriel pour donner de la lumière aux couchages du bas. Même les chiens qui ont leur propre petite maison avec ascenseur ont été pris en compte dans cette demeure toute en nuances.

Lela Rose chose all the furniture for the living spaces, including the white sofa by Edward Wormley, the circular banquet by Pierre Paulin, and the red chair by Maurizio Galante.

Lela Rose wählte sämtliche Möbel im Wohnbereich selbst aus, unter anderem das Sofa von Edward Wormley, das runde Sitzelement von Pierre Paulin und den roten Stuhl von Maurizio Galante.

Lela Rose a choisi tout le mobilier des espaces à vivre, y compris le canapé blanc d'Edward Wormley, la banquette circulaire de Pierre Paulin et le fauteuil rouge de Maurizio Galante.

A bamboo-lined box leading to the dining area contains built-in motorized tables that rise from the floor. The kitchen/ dining area features unique tables that can be joined together for huge dinners.

Ein mit Bambusholz verkleideter offener Kubus, der zum Essbereich führt, verfügt über Tische, die im Boden versenkt werden können. Der Küchen- und Essbereich ist gekennzeichnet durch einzelne Tische, die bei großen Abendessen zusammengestellt werden.

Un box revêtu de bambou menant à la saille à manger contient des tables motorisées encastrées qui surgissent du plancher. L'espace cuisine/salle à manger contient des tables uniques qui peuvent se réunir en une seule lors des grands dîners.

The below-ground master bedroom opens onto a small private courtyard.

Das unten liegende Elternschlafzimmer bietet einen Blick auf den kleinen privaten Innenhof.

La chambre en sous-sol s'ouvre sur une petite cour privée.

The architects installed a vertical skylight to let daylight into the bedroom levels and a massive closet on the lowest level.

Die Architekten ließen ein senkrechtes Oberlicht einbauen, damit Tageslicht in die Etage mit den Schlafzimmern fällt, und einen großen begehbaren Kleiderschrank im untersten Stockwerk.

Les architectes ont installé une lucarne verticale pour faire entrer la lumière du jour dans les chambres des différents niveaux et un immense placard dans le niveau du bas.

Frosted glass walls and ceiling allow light to permeate the airy baths on the lower floors as well.

Wände und Decken aus Milchglas ermöglichen ebenfalls, dass Licht durch die luftigen Bäder in die unteren Etagen dringen kann.

Les murs et le plafond en verre givré laissent passer la lumière qui imprègne aussi les salles de bains aérées des étages en dessous.

On Top of the World
Midtown East

WITH WINDOWS OPENING to sweeping vistas of Manhattan, it isn't surprising that this 3,000-square-foot residence's owner wanted interiors emphasizing its views. Perched atop the Trump World Tower, the two-bedroom co-op is the owner's primary residence, so he turned to designer Mark Cunningham to give it warmth and sophistication befitting a full-time home. Gleaning color cues from the skyline, the designer cultivated "a sleek, masculine penthouse in the sky" with diverse materials, including lacquer, stone, and burnished metals in camel, charcoal, and black spiked with shots of red. The cohesive luxury begins in the living room, where a leather sectional embraces the spectacular view. Art and accents lend playful pops of flavor. Vintage-modern furnishings, such as the 1970s chrome bar stools in the kitchen, round out the mix with touches of retro glamour.

DER BESITZER DIESER 280 Quadratmeter großen Wohnung wollte die Innenräume so gestaltet haben, dass sie die fantastischen Ausblicke auf Manhattan unterstreichen. Das Apartment mit zwei Schlafzimmern im oberen Stockwerk des Trump World Towers ist der Hauptwohnsitz des Eigentümers, der sich an den Innenarchitekten Mark Cunningham wandte, um ihm Wärme und Raffinesse zu verleihen. Der Designer richtete sich farblich nach der Skyline und schuf mit verschiedenen Materialien, darunter Lack, Stein und poliertes kamelfarbenes, dunkelgraues und rot gesprenkeltes schwarzes Metall „ein glattes, maskulines Penthouse im Himmel". Der stimmige Luxus beginnt im Wohnzimmer, in dem sich von der Couchgarnitur aus Leder ein spektakuläres Panorama bietet. Kunst und die unterschiedlich gesetzten Akzente verleihen dem Raum auf spielerische Weise atmosphärische Glanzlichter. Moderne Vintage-Möbel wie die Chrom-Barstühle in der Küche aus den 1970er-Jahren runden die Mischung mit einem Hauch von Retroglamour ab.

AVEC DES FENÊTRES qui donnent sur une vue panoramique de Manhattan, rien de surprenant à ce que le propriétaire de cette résidence de 280 mètres carrés ait souhaité avoir des intérieurs qui mettent en valeur la vue. Perché au sommet de la Trump World Tower, cet appartement en copropriété de deux chambres est la résidence principale du propriétaire et donc il s'est tourné vers le décorateur Mark Cunningham pour donner de la chaleur et un raffinement tel qu'il convient à une demeure à plein temps. Le décorateur s'est inspiré de la ligne d'horizon pour ses tonalités et a produit un « penthouse chic et masculin dans le ciel » à l'aide de divers matériaux comme la laque, la pierre et des métaux brunis en tons caramel, anthracite et noir entrelacés de giclées de rouge. Cet ensemble de luxe commence dans le séjour où un canapé d'angle en cuir donne sur une vue spectaculaire. Des œuvres d'art et des touches décoratives ajoutent un ton ludique et savoureux. Des meubles vintages modernes comme les tabourets de bar en chrome des années 1970 dans la cuisine complètent l'ensemble avec des touches rétro-glamour.

An art glass vase by Barovier & Toso (previous page) filled with magnolia leaves sets off the console. Down-lighters designed by Angelo Mangiarotti circa 1962 highlight the dining table.

Eine Glaskunstvase von Barovier & Toso (vorige Seite), gefüllt mit Magnolienblättern, hebt die Konsole hervor. Deckenleuchten, von Angelo Mangiarotti um 1962 entworfen, weisen auf den Esstisch.

Un magnifique vase en verre de Barovier & Toso (page précédente) rempli de feuilles de magnolia définit la console. Des lumières descendantes conçues par Angelo Mangiarotti en 1962 illuminent la grande table.

A Richard Serra work punctuates the wall behind the living room's curved sofa. On the coffee table sits a glass vase by Franco Deboni from Bernd Goeckler Antiques.

Ein Werk von Richard Serra unterstreicht die Wand hinter dem geschwungenen Sofa im Wohnzimmer. Auf dem Couchtisch steht eine Franco-Deboni-Glasvase von Bernd Goeckler Antiques.

Une œuvre de Richard Serra accentue le mur derrière le canapé en ligne courbe du salon. Sur la petite table se trouve un vase en verre signé Franco Deboni venant de Bernd Goeckler Antiques.

Parisian Refuge
Brooklyn

HAVING LIVED FOR years in France, this Brooklyn home's owners had a taste for French design. When they moved into a 4,500-square-foot townhouse, they hoped to create a dwelling that would remind them of their life in Paris. After enlisting architect Claude Puaux to recreate its exterior with French limestone, they turned to designer Kathryn Scott to infuse its interiors with classic French touches. "The budget was not endless, and the aspirations were high," says Scott. Among the must-haves were a Tischler und Sohn windowed door, Guerin hardware, and Viking kitchen appliances. The owners also desired custom furnishings, including the marble coffee table in the living room and a cerused oak desk in the master bedroom. Working with artisans for custom work meant the process took time—almost four years. But the finished product—a blend of traditional French detailing and classic modern touches—was clearly worth the wait.

NACH JAHREN IN Frankreich hatten die Besitzer dieses Hauses in Brooklyn eine Vorliebe für französisches Design entwickelt. Als sie in dieses 420 Quadratmeter große Stadthaus zogen, sollte es sie an ihr Leben in Paris erinnern. Nachdem sie Claude Puaux beauftragt hatten, die Außenfassade mit französischem Kalkstein zu verkleiden, wandten sie sich an die Innenarchitektin Kathryn Scott, um den Innenräumen eine französische Note zu verleihen. „Das Budget war begrenzt und die Erwartungen hoch", erklärt Scott. Auf der Wunschliste ganz oben standen eine Fenstertür von Tischler und Sohn, Armaturen und Beschläge von Guerin und Küchengeräte von Viking. Die Besitzer wünschten sich ebenfalls eine maßgeschneiderte Einrichtung, unter anderem den Marmorcouchtisch im Wohnzimmer und einen Schreibtisch aus gekalkter Eiche im großen Schlafzimmer. Durch die Zusammenarbeit mit Kunsthandwerkern nahm die Ausgestaltung des Hauses einige Zeit in Anspruch – fast vier Jahre. Doch das Ergebnis – eine Mischung aus traditionellen französischen Details und klassisch-modernen Elementen – war das Warten eindeutig wert.

AYANT VÉCU EN France, les propriétaires de cette résidence ont acquis le goût de la décoration française. À leur retour dans une maison de ville de près de 420 mètres carrés, ils s'attachèrent à créer une demeure qui leur rappelerait leur vie à Paris. Après avoir fait appel à l'architecte Claude Puaux pour recréer un extérieur en pierre de tuffeau, ils se tournèrent vers la décoratrice Kathryn Scott pour apporter des touches françaises classiques aux intérieurs. « Le budget n'était pas illimité et les aspirations visaient très haut », nous dit Kathryn. Parmi les objets incontournables figuraient une porte vitrée de Tischler und Sohn, des ferrures Guérin et des électroménagers Viking. Les propriétaires voulaient aussi des meubles sur mesure, comme la table en marbre du salon et un bureau en bois de chêne cérusé dans la chambre principale. Comme il fallait travailler avec des artisans qui faisaient du sur mesure, il a fallu du temps pour transformer la maison — presque quatre ans. Mais le produit fini, un mélange de style français avec des touches modernes classiques valait la peine de patienter.

Amid a soothing neutral palette, classic architectural elements, such as the 18-foot-tall windowed door in the living room, bronze stair rails in the breakfast room, and cerused oak cabinets in the kitchen bring French flair to this Brooklyn townhouse.

Die sich in einer beruhigenden, neutralen Farbpalette einfügenden klassischen Architekturelemente, wie eine 6 Meter hohe Fenstertür im Wohnzimmer, ein Treppengeländer aus Bronze im Frühstücksraum und gekalkte Eichenschränke in der Küche, verleihen diesem Stadthaus in Brooklyn französisches Flair.

Dans une palette de tons neutres et apaisants, des éléments architecturaux classiques comme une porte vitrée de 6 mètres de haut dans le salon, des rampes d'escalier en bronze dans la salle du déjeuner et des rangements en bois de chêne cérusé dans la cuisine donnent un air français à cette maison de ville à Brooklyn.

Designer Kathryn Scott custom-designed the upholstered benches to follow the lines
of the tree-slab dining table. Extra-high baseboard moldings and a bronze rail accent
the staircase.

Die Innenarchitektin Kathryn Scott entwarf die extra angefertigten gepolsterten Bänke
und passte sie der geschwungenen Form der Baumplatte des Esstisches an. Besonders
hohe Sockelfriese und ein Bronzegeländer akzentuieren die Treppe.

La décoratrice Kathryn Scott a conçu sur mesure les banquettes tapissées pour
qu'elles s'accordent avec les lignes de la grande table constituée par une dalle en bois.
Des plinthes avec moulures très hautes et une rampe en bronze accentuent l'escalier.

The bathroom cabinets are all lined with white marble. Completely uncluttered, all of the rooms, including the bedrooms, contain no unnecessary furniture and the colors throughout are variations on white.

Die Badezimmerschränke sind alle mit weißem Marmor verkleidet. In sämtlichen Räumen, einschließlich der Badezimmer, wurde auf überflüssige Möbel verzichtet. Sie zeichnen sich durch ihre klare Struktur aus. Die eingesetzten Farben sind durchweg Varianten von Weiß.

Les armoires de la salle de bains sont toutes recouvertes de marbre blanc. Sans aucun fatras inutile, toutes les chambres, y compris les chambres à coucher ne contiennent pas de mobilier superflu et les couleurs sont toujours en camaïeux de blancs.

Rooms With a View
TriBeCa

RARE IS THE Manhattan apartment with truly spectacular views, but this 5,000-square-foot TriBeCa loft boasts them in all four directions. "The skyline is the backdrop to every room in this apartment," says interior designer Carol Egan. Working with the owners' collection of mostly modern Danish ceramics as accents, she set the tone with "a happy and sophisticated palette of colors and a range of textures." One of the first things Egan selected was the fabric for the living room sofas—a 1968 design by Paule Leleu—which determined the color scheme. She also reinvented traditional elements with a modern twist. Bespoke textiles from Paris and London bring warm notes to the bedroom. Invariably, another issue in loft spaces is storage. The designer rose to the challenge with built-in millwork cabinets and shelves, which keep clutter contained and the views open and clear.

EINE WOHNUNG MIT wirklich spektakulären Blicken ist selten in Manhattan, doch dieses 460 Quadratmeter große Loft in TriBeCa bietet sie in alle vier Himmelsrichtungen. „Die Skyline bildet in sämtlichen Zimmern dieser Wohnung die Kulisse", erklärt Innenarchitektin Carol Egan. Mit denen von ihr gesetzten Akzenten, für die sie meistenteils auf die Sammlung moderner dänischer Keramik zurückgriff, legte sie eine „fröhliche, raffinierte Farbpalette und eine Reihe von Texturen" fest. Egan wählte anfangs unter anderem den Stoff für die Sofas im Wohnzimmer aus – ein Design von Paule Leleu aus dem Jahr 1968 –, durch den das Farbschema bestimmt wurde. Außerdem erfand sie traditionelle Elemente neu und versah sie mit einer modernen Interpretation. Die maßgeschneiderten Stoffe aus Paris und London verleihen dem Schlafzimmer eine warme Note. Eine weitere Frage, die sich stets bei Lofts stellt, ist das Thema der Aufbewahrung. Die Innenarchitektin meisterte diese Herausforderung, indem sie Holzschränke und -regale einbauen ließ, wodurch Ordnung geschaffen wurde und die Ausblicke unverstellt bleiben.

RARES SONT LES appartements à Manhattan qui offrent une vue vraiment spectaculaire mais ce loft de près de 460 mètres carrés dans TriBeCa tient ses promesses et dans les quatre directions. « La ligne d'horizon est la toile de fond de chacune des pièces de l'appartement », explique la décoratrice Carol Egan. Tirant parti de la collection de céramiques avant tout de style danois moderne pour les touches décoratives, elle a donné le ton avec « une palette de couleurs joyeuse et raffinée et toute une série de textures ». Un des premiers choix d'Egan fut le tissu pour les canapés du séjour, un dessin de Paule Leleu datant de 1968 et qui fut le point de départ pour les coloris. Elle a aussi réinventé des éléments traditionnels pour leur donner une allure moderne. Des textiles spécialement commandés de Paris et Londres apportent un ton chaleureux à la chambre. Et comme d'habitude les rangements étant un des problèmes des espaces loft, la décoratrice a su relever le défi avec des armoires et rayons encastrés en menuiserie préfabriquée pour éviter le désordre et permettre une vue claire et dégagée.

A lamp by David Weeks hangs over the dining table. Carol Egan designed the bold living room sofas.

Eine Lampe von David Weeks hängt über dem Esstisch. Carol Egan entwarf die auffälligen Sofas im Wohnzimmer.

Une lampe de David Weeks pend au-dessus de la grande table. Carol Egan a conçu les canapés audacieux du séjour.

Walnut and white lacquer cabinets house a collection of Danish ceramics. A Donald Baechler screen print provides a spirited backdrop for a Jens Risom chair and ottoman.

In Schränken aus Walnussholz und weißem Lack befindet sich eine Sammlung dänischer Keramik. Ein Siebdruck von Donald Baechler bildet einen lebendigen Hintergrund für einen Sessel und einen Polsterhocker von Jens Risom.

Les armoires laquées en noyer et blanc abritent une collection de céramiques danoises. Un paravent de Donald Baechler offre une toile de fond dynamique pour un fauteuil et un pouf de Jens Risom.

Wallpaper by Madeleine Castaing softens the master bedroom's niche. Hans Wegner's Papa Bear Chair *offers a place to perch to enjoy the view.*

Eine Tapete von Madeleine Castaing fügt sich sanft in die Nische des großen Schlafzimmers ein. Der „Papa Bear Chair" von Hans Wegner bietet sich dazu an, die Aussicht zu genießen.

Le papier peint de Madeleine Castaing donne un air douillet au coin de la chambre principale. La chaise papa ours de Hans Wegner invite à se percher pour profiter de la vue.

Index

Biographies

Jean Nayar

A CONTRIBUTOR TO numerous national and regional publications, including *Luxe*, *Interior Design*, *Hamptons*, and *Ocean Drive* magazines, Jean Nayar writes about architecture, art, and design and is the author of several books, including *Green Living By Design* and *The Happy Home Project*, both published by Filipacchi Publishing. Her books and insights on design and real estate have been featured in *The New York Times*, *The Washington Post*, and other newspapers, magazines, and Web sites. She is additionally a real estate agent with Sotheby's International Realty and splits her time between New York and Miami Beach with her husband.

JEAN NAYAR SCHREIBT für zahlreiche Zeitschriften über Architektur, Kunst und Innenarchitektur, unter anderem für *Luxe*, *Interior Design*, *Hamptons* und *Ocean Drive*. Darüber hinaus ist sie Autorin verschiedener Bücher, darunter *Green Living By Design* und *The Happy Home Project*, beide erschienen bei Filipacchi Publishing. Ihre Bücher und Erkenntnisse zur Innenarchitektur und zu Immobilien wurden in der *New York Times*, der *Washington Post* und anderen Zeitungen, Zeitschriften und Webseiten besprochen. Sie ist außerdem als Immobilienmaklerin für Sotheby's International Realty tätig und teilt sich zusammen mit ihrem Mann ihre Zeit zwischen New York und Miami Beach auf.

JEAN NAYAR ÉCRIT dans de nombreuses publications nationales et régionales comme les magazines *Luxe*, *Interior Design*, *Hamptons* et *Ocean Drive* sur l'architecture, l'art et le design et elle est l'auteur de plusieurs livres dont *Green Living By Design* (Vie verte par conception) et *The Happy Home Project* (Projet maison heureuse) tous deux publiés par Filipacchi Publishing. Ses livres et ses idées sur le design et l'immobilier ont été commentés dans le *New York Times*, le *Washington Post* et d'autres journaux, magazines et sites web. Elle est aussi agent immobilier chez Sotheby's International Realty et partage son temps entre New York et Miami Beach avec son mari.

Vanessa Weiner von Bismarck

BORN IN HAMBURG and educated in Germany and the United Kingdom, Vanessa Weiner von Bismarck first worked in London as a sugar trader. In 1999, she moved to New York and founded BPCM, a public relations agency, with Carrie Ellen Phillips. Today von Bismarck spends her time between Europe and the United States and is married to Maximilian Weiner, a healthcare entrepreneur, and has two sons named Laszlo and Cosmo.

VANESSA WEINER VON Bismarck, geboren in Hamburg, ausgebildet in Deutschland und dem Vereinigten Königreich, arbeitete zunächst als Zuckerhändlerin in London. 1999 zog sie nach New York und gründete zusammen mit Carrie Ellen Phillips die PR-Agentur BPCM. Heute verbringt von Bismarck ihre Zeit sowohl in Europa als auch den Vereinigten Staaten. Sie ist mit Maximilian Weiner, einem Unternehmer aus der Gesundheitsbranche, verheiratet und hat zwei Söhne, Lazlo und Cosmo.

NÉE À HAMBOURG, Vanessa Weiner von Bismarck a grandi en Allemagne et au Royaume-Uni et elle a d'abord travaillé à Londres comme négociante en sucre. Elle partit pour New York en 1999 et fonda BPCM, une agence de relations publiques, avec Carrie Ellen Phillips. Aujourd'hui von Bismarck partage son temps entre l'Europe et les États-Unis. Elle est mariée avec Maximilian Weiner, entrepreneur en santé, et a deux fils qui s'appellent Laszlo et Cosmo.

Credits & Imprint

Edited by Vanessa Weiner von Bismarck
Texts by Jean Nayar
Editorial coordination by Victorine Lamothe
Design by Allison Stern
Production by Nele Jansen, teNeues Verlag
Photography coordination by
Sandra Kaltenhausser
Color separation by MT Vreden
Translations by:
  Irene Eisenhut (German)
  Helena Solodky-Wang (French)

teNeues Publishing Group
Kempen
Berlin
Cologne
Düsseldorf
Hamburg
London
Munich
New York
Paris

teNeues

Published by teNeues Publishing Group
teNeues Verlag GmbH + Co. KG
Am Selder 37, 47906 Kempen, Germany
Phone: +49 (0)2152 916 0, Fax: +49 (0)2152 916 111
e-mail: books@teneues.de

Press Department: Andrea Rehn
Phone: +49 (0)2152 916 202
e-mail: arehn@teneues.de

teNeues Digital Media GmbH
Kohlfurter Straße 41–43, 10999 Berlin, Germany
Phone: +49 (0)30 700 77 65 0

teNeues Publishing Company
7 West 18th Street, New York, NY 10011, USA
Phone: +1 212 627 9090, Fax: +1 212 627 9511

teNeues Publishing UK Ltd.
12 Ferndene Road, London SE24 0AQ, UK
Phone: +44 (0)20 3542 8997

teNeues France S.A.R.L.
39, rue des Billets, 18250 Henrichemont, France
Phone: +33 (0)2 4826 9348, Fax: +33 (0)1 7072 3482

www.teneues.com

© 2014 teNeues Verlag GmbH + Co. KG, Kempen
ISBN: 978-3-8327-9804-8
Library of Congress Control Number: 2013957666

Printed in the Czech Republic.